SPANISH EVERY DAY

A Learning Adventure for Young Readers

Second Edition

William C. Harvey

Illustrations: Dre Design
Denise Gilgannon

BARRON'S

For Valerie and Joanna

Published by Kaplan, Inc., d/b/a Barron's Educational Series
750 Third Avenue
New York, NY 10017
www.barronseduc.com

ISBN: 978-0-7641-4596-4 (book only)
ISBN: 978-1-4380-7050-6 (book and CD set)

Library of Congress Catalog Card Number 2010937936

Manufactured by Bind-Rite Robbinsville, LLC, Robbinsville, NJ
Date of Manufacture: September 2016

9 8

Kaplan, Inc., d/b/a Barron's Educational Series print books are available at
special quantity discounts to use for sales promotions, employee premiums,
or educational purposes. For more information or to purchase books, please
call the Simon & Schuster special sales department at 866-506-1949.

CONTENTS

ABOUT THE AUTHOR
William C. Harvey is the author of many books, and has been teaching both Spanish and English for more than 20 years. His books and classes are fun because he makes learning easy for everyone. He wrote *Spanish Every Day* because he wanted boys and girls to know how exciting learning Spanish can be!

A NOTE TO PARENTS
Remind your young readers of the special features found in *Spanish Every Day*. They are located at the back of the book:

English-Spanish Vocabulary Lists
Cutout Vocabulary Flashcards

If you purchased the book and CD kit, make sure that they listen to the CDs as often as possible. They are easy to follow along, since all Spanish words are practiced on the CDs in the same order that they are presented in the book.

1 CHAPTER
UNO

Aprendamos español

(Let's Learn Spanish)

YOUR NEW FRIEND

This is Mister *Amigo*. He speaks both SPANISH and English. You can find him on many pages in this book. He will give you secrets about SPANISH, so that you can learn it easily—and very fast! Why don't you color him and all the drawings in this book?

ABOUT THIS BOOK

Today is a very special day. You are going to learn a new language called SPANISH.

The language you speak is called English. But many people in the world don't speak English. They speak other languages—like French, Chinese, or SPANISH!

This book will teach you how to understand and speak SPANISH. If you learn a little SPANISH every day, soon you will know two languages instead of one!

ABOUT THE CDs

This book is sold with or without CDs. If you got it with the CDs, listen to them as you read this book, and stop them when you finish reading. Don't worry, the CDs will tell you the page number!

Here are the many countries where people speak SPANISH.
Each country has a number. Take a pencil and draw a line from
the number of the country you see on the map to the same
number on the list. You *may* ask for help!

SPAIN (1)
MEXICO (2)
CUBA (3)
DOMINICAN REPUBLIC (4)
ARGENTINA (5)
GUATEMALA (6)
PERU (7)

EL SALVADOR (8)
COLOMBIA (9)
BOLIVIA (10)
URUGUAY (11)
CHILE (12)
COSTA RICA (13)
PUERTO RICO (14)

ECUADOR (15)
NICARAGUA (16)
HONDURAS (17)
VENEZUELA (18)
PARAGUAY (19)
PANAMA (20)

This book also has a VOCABULARY LIST of SPANISH and ENGLISH words. Whenever you forget how to say something, you can look it up in the VOCABULARY LIST, which is found at the back of this book.

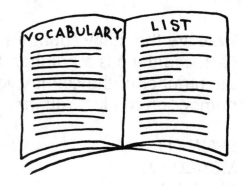

Start now by looking up the word "SPANISH." Write the word here:

_____

(To check your answer, look at the upside-down word below)

ANSWER: español

Good! Now, are you all set to learn more about the SPANISH language?

Let's begin with the most important part of all . . .

THE SUPER SOUNDS OF SPANISH

These are the five most important sounds of SPANISH. Once you learn them, you will be able to understand, speak, and read SPANISH words correctly.

The letters look just like English, but in SPANISH they have a very different sound. Go ahead, say each one aloud three times.

A (like "ah") The doctor tells the boy to say "ah."

E (like "eh") The man who cannot hear well says "eh."

I (like "ee") The girl who is scared says "ee."

O (like "oh") The lady who is surprised says "oh."

U (like "oo") At night the owl says "oo."

Here's what these SUPER SOUNDS look like inside SPANISH words. Can you say each one correctly?

amigo

mucho

grande

Do you know what these words mean in English?
Look them up in the VOCABULARY LIST if you need to.

Let's learn some other sounds in SPANISH.
Practice each word three times, and notice what it means in English!

The letter **J** sounds like an "H," like in the word <u>**happy**</u>.

jabón soap

jirafa giraffe

juego game

The letter **H** in Spanish has no sound at all:

<u>*h*</u>*ola* hello

<u>*h*</u>*uevo* egg

<u>*h*</u>*ombre* man

The letter **Z** sounds just like an "S":

lu<u>*z*</u> light

<u>*z*</u>*apato* shoe

man<u>*z*</u>*ana* apple

And the letter **V** in SPANISH sounds more like a "B":

pa<u>*v*</u>*o* turkey

<u>*v*</u>*estido* dress

<u>*v*</u>*aca* cow

Remember that people will understand you even if your words aren't perfect, so just do the best you can!

Go ahead—write the correct SPANISH word next to each picture:

_____

_____

_____

_____

Some SPANISH sounds are a little harder to say. These letters look funny, so be careful when you read each word aloud:

The SPANISH letter **LL** sounds a lot like a "Y," like in the word **yes**.

amarillo yellow

silla chair

caballo horse

The SPANISH letter **ñ** sounds like "NY" in the word "CA<u>NY</u>ON":

Señorita (Srta.)
young lady (Ms.)

Señora (Sra.)
lady (Mrs.)

Señor (Sr.)
man (Mr.)

When together, the letters **QU** sound like a "K":

poquito a little bit

chiquito tiny

chaqueta jacket

Let's practice. You learned all of these words earlier. Fill in the missing letters, and then read everything aloud:

po__u__ __o   cha__ __ et__

a__ari__ __o   si __ __ a

__spa__ol   ca__al__o

__hiq__ __ to   s__ño__a

__est__do   j__eg__

8

RR is another letter in SPANISH that is very different from ENGLISH. To say it right, you must "roll your Rs," which sounds a lot like a car motor—RRRRRR!! Try to read these words the best you can:

*ca**rr**o* car

*pe**rr**o* dog

*bu**rr**o* donkey

Look at this funny picture. Name everything you see in SPANISH:

ANSWERS: perro, vestido, carro, vaca, pavo

Look how some SPANISH words have a little slanted line over a letter, like this ó. This tells us *to say that part of the word louder* than the other parts.

María	**Mary**
José	**Joe**
adiós	**good-bye**

1. **SPANISH words are pronounced exactly the way they are written.**

2. **Knowing the vowels (A, E, I, O, and U) is the secret to understanding and speaking SPANISH.**

3. **People will still understand you even if you don't say every SPANISH word correctly.**

4. **Say the accented (') part of a word a little louder. When the SPANISH word has no written accent, it is spoken louder at the end, unless it ends in A, E, I, O, U, N, or S.**

5. **REMEMBER: Your SPANISH will get better only if you speak it EVERY DAY . . !!**

SPANISH WORDS YOU ALREADY KNOW

These next words are fun to practice because they are exactly the same in both languages. But remember—they sound different when you say them in *español*:

doctor doctor
animal animal
color color

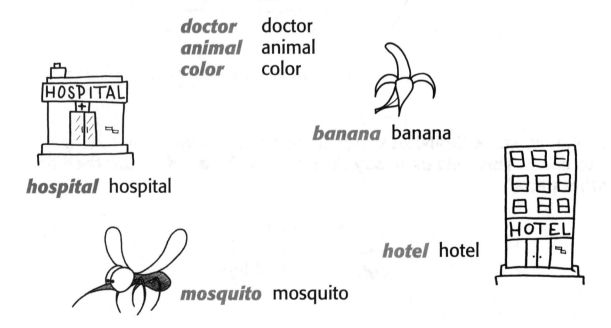

banana banana

hospital hospital

hotel hotel

mosquito mosquito

10

Let's keep reading aloud. Say all of these SPANISH words correctly:

taco   *Los Angeles*
rodeo   *Florida*
salsa   *San Francisco*
chocolate   *Colorado*
tortilla   *Nevada*

If you're having trouble, be sure to review pages 5 through 9.

Now, underline all the SPANISH words you can find in the story below:

Juan is a doctor at a hospital in Los Angeles. He loves big tortilla tacos with lots of salsa. His favorite hotel in Florida sells chocolate bananas. He listens to the rodeo on the radio when he goes to Colorado.

EASY SPANISH WORDS

Look at this list of SPANISH words. Most people learn them first because they are easy to remember:

nada	nothing
sí	yes
amigo	friend
mucho	a lot
gracias	thank you
bueno	good
grande	big

adiós good-bye

agua water

dinero money

casa house

fiesta party

chico small

You saw these words before. Can you remember what they mean?

señorita	<u>young lady</u>
hola	_____
zapato	_____
hombre	_____
carro	_____

ANSWERS: hello, shoe, man, car

12

This time, connect each word with its opposite:

chico	*sí*
hola	*señora*
poquito	*grande*
no	*adiós*
señor	*mucho*

ANSWERS: *chico—grande, hola—adiós, poco—mucho, no—sí, señor—señora*

Practice by putting whole sentences together. You can do it! For example:

Es mucho dinero.	It's a lot of money.
La casa es grande.	The house is big.
¡Gracias y adiós!	Thanks and good-bye!

WHAT'S YOUR NAME IN SPANISH?

Did you know that kids' names in SPANISH are different than in English? Read this list of people's names in SPANISH and practice every sound. If your name is not on the list, it's still okay; most people who speak SPANISH will call you by your real name anyway!

Los Nombres
(Names)

Los niños
(Boys)

Bobby	*Roberto*
Charlie	*Carlos*
Eddie	*Eduardo*
Frank	*Francisco*
George	*Jorge*
Jerry	*Geraldo*

Henry	*Enrique*
Jimmy	*Jaime*
John	*Juan*
Mark	*Marcos*
Nick	*Nicolás*
Tony	*Antonio*
Mike	*Miguel*
Peter	*Pedro*
Joey	*José*
Richard	*Ricardo*
Paul	*Pablo*
Steven	*Esteban*
Billy	*Guillermo*
Fred	*Federico*
Tom	*Tomás*
Andy	*Andrés*
Matthew	*Mateo*

Las niñas
(Girls)

Alice	*Alicia*
Betty	*Beatriz*
Anne	*Ana*
Carol	*Carolina*
Ellen	*Elena*
Jane	*Juana*
Cathy	*Catalina*
Susan	*Susana*
Lynn	*Lina*
Margaret	*Margarita*
Sarah	*Sara*
Hope	*Esperanza*
Lucy	*Luz*
Christy	*Cristina*
Mary	*María*
Grace	*Graciela*
Eve	*Eva*
Valerie	*Valeria*
Rose	*Rosa*
Julie	*Julia*

Watch out for these SPANISH names—they look just like English, but they are pronounced differently!

Daniel   **David**
Gloria   **Laura**
Samuel   **Víctor**
Linda   **Patricia**

Learn how to ask for people's names in SPANISH. Try this with someone right away!

What's your name?   *¿Cómo te llamas?*
My name is . . .   *Me llamo . . .*

MORE THINGS TO SAY IN *ESPAÑOL*

Speak a different language with your family and friends! Say these things today in SPANISH instead of English:

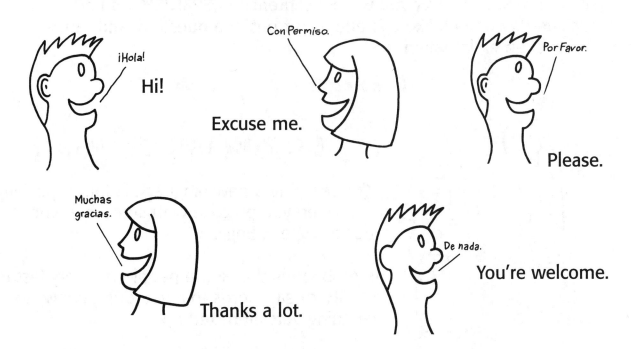

¡Hola!
Hi!

Con Permiso.
Excuse me.

Por Favor.
Please.

Muchas gracias.
Thanks a lot.

De nada.
You're welcome.

Here's a whole conversation! And you can say it and understand it!

How are you?

Very well, thanks. And you?

What's going on?

Not much.

Good-bye!

See you later!

By the way, whenever you write a sentence in SPANISH, add an upside-down mark like this one: ¿ in front of a question, and ¡ in front of an exclamation.

¿Cómo estás?   **¡Bien!**

DO YOU UNDERSTAND?

Learning a new language is fun, especially when you practice with someone who doesn't speak English.

The problem is that some people talk very fast in SPANISH, or say words that you don't know, so everything gets all mixed up.

Here are some things you can say in SPANISH so that everybody will understand one another:

I'm sorry.   *Lo siento.*

Please speak more slowly.   *Habla más despacio, por favor.*

I'm learning SPANISH.   *Estoy aprendiendo español.*

I speak a little.   *Hablo un poco.*

Do you speak Spanish?

Do you understand?

Do you know?

I don't understand.

I don't know.

I don't remember.

To learn more things to say in SPANISH, look at the VOCABULARY LIST at the end of the book.

Don't forget these:

Good morning	*Buenos días.*
Good afternoon.	*Buenas tardes.*
Good night.	*Buenas noches.*

Let's practice some more:

Put SPANISH words in these balloons, and make the people
talk to each other!

Now, connect the words that go together best.
And when you're done, read all of your answers aloud!

¡Hasta luego!	*Me llamo José.*
Muchas gracias.	*Muy bien.*
¿Cómo estás?	*Sin novedad.*
¿Qué pasa?	*¡Adiós!*
¿Hablas español?	*Sí, un poco.*
¿Cómo te llamas?	*De nada.*

ANSWERS: *¡Hasta luego!—¡Adiós! Muchas gracias.—De nada. ¿Cómo estás?—Muy bien. ¿Cómo te llamas?—Me llamo José. ¿Hablas español?—Sí, un poco. ¿Qué pasa?—Sin novedad.*

Did you get them all correct? *¡Bueno!* If you had trouble, go back and read Chapter *UNO* again.

Look at these expressions. How many can you memorize at once?
How many will you remember after reading them three times?

I hope so!	*¡Ojalá!*
I'm so glad!	*¡Me alegro!*
Maybe!	*¡Quizás!*
Me, neither!	*¡Yo tampoco!*
Me, too!	*¡Yo también!*
More or less!	*¡Más o menos!*
Of course!	*¡Por supuesto!*
Really?	*¿Verdad?*
That's OK!	*¡Está bien!*
I think so!	*¡Creo que sí!*

Whenever you're ready, go on to
Chapter *DOS*. It's time for you
to speak more SPANISH every day!

2 CHAPTER
DOS

En mi cuarto

(In My Room)

It's time to get up and speak SPANISH! When you wake up in the morning, what do you see?

pillow	*la almohada*
sheet	*la sábana*
bedspread	*la cubrecama*
pajamas	*el pijama*
clothes	*la ropa*

bed *la cama*

book *el libro*

blanket *la frazada*

stuffed animal
el animal de peluche

toy *el juguete*

Let's stop for a moment. Try making your bed in SPANISH!
Unscramble these letters and practice each word:

la básaan _____

la acbaecrum _____

la maac _____

la zdaaarf _____

la halamdao _____

Go to your bedroom, and point to these things:

bookshelf   *el librero*
lamp   *la lámpara*
floor   *el piso*
chair   *la silla*
wall   *la pared*
ceiling   *el techo*

closet *el ropero*

window *la ventana*

table *la mesa*

door *la puerta*

dresser *el tocador*

clock *el reloj*

What Is *el* and What Is *la*?

Did you notice that in SPANISH the word *el* or *la* appears in front of words that name people and things?

Most of the time, words that end with *o* have *el* in front . . .

el libr<u>o</u>   el pis<u>o</u>   el diner<u>o</u>   el amig<u>o</u>   el pav<u>o</u>

. . . while words that end in *a* have *la* in front:

la señor<u>a</u>   la cam<u>a</u>   la jiraf<u>a</u>   la cas<u>a</u>   la banan<u>a</u>

And what do *el* and *la* mean? They mean "the"!

Put *el* or *la* in front of these other words, and then write the English:

<u>el</u> *juego*   <u>the game</u>

___ *manzana*   _____

___ *zapato*   _____

___ *huevo*   _____

___ *chaqueta*   _____

___ *vaca*   _____

___ *carro*   _____

ANSWERS: la manzana — apple
el zapato — shoe
el huevo — egg
la chaqueta — jacket
la vaca — cow
el carro — car

23

uno

dos

tres

cuatro

cinco

seis

siete

ocho

nueve

diez

Los números
(Numbers)

Learn the numbers in SPANISH, and you can count everything around you in two languages! Start with the numbers 1 to 10:

Fill in the missing number in SPANISH:

<u>tres</u> lámparas

_ _ _ _ _ _ camas

_ _ _ _ _ sillas

ANSWERS: *cinco camas, ocho sillas*

24

Now let's practice more *números* in SPANISH:

11	*once*
12	*doce*
13	*trece*
14	*catorce*
15	*quince*
16	*dieciséis*
17	*diecisiete*
18	*dieciocho*
19	*diecinueve*
20	*veinte*

Now that you know some *números*, try out this question right away!

How old are you?   I'm . . .
¿Cuántos años tienes?   *Tengo . . .*

Write your age in SPANISH here: _____

ANSWERS: *uno dos tres cuatro cinco*
seis siete ocho nueve diez
once doce trece catorce quince
dieciséis diecisiete dieciocho
diecinueve veinte

_____ _____ _____ _____ _____

_____ _____ _____ _____ _____

_____ _____ _____ _____ _____

_____ _____

These numbers are all mixed up. Take a minute to put them in order. And be sure to read them aloud!

diez *uno* *veinte* *dieciocho* *doce* *tres*

ocho *quince* *diecisiete* *cuatro* *nueve*

dieciséis *dos* *cinco* *catorce* *siete*

once *diecinueve* *seis* *trece*

Los juguetes
(Toys)

Do you have any toys in your bedroom? Be sure to count them in *español*!

game	*el juego*
puzzle	*el rompecabezas*
kite	*la cometa*
blocks	*los bloques*
robot	*el robot*
bat	*el bate*
ball	*la pelota*
glove	*el guante*
drum	*el tambor*
airplane	*el avión*
skates	*los patines*

balloon *el globo*

spaceship
la nave espacial

doll *la muñeca*

soldier *el soldado*

train *el tren*

truck *el camión*

guitar *la guitarra*

ship *el barco*

skateboard *la patineta*

car *el carro*

bicycle *la bicicleta*

You can also have fun with one of these:

computer *la computadora*

stereo *el estéreo*

DVD *el devedé*

Look for these toys in the WORD SEARCH puzzle below.

ESTEREO	**PATINETA**	**BICICLETA**
PELOTA	**GUANTE**	**TAMBOR**
JUEGO	**GLOBO**	**BATE**
SOLDADO	**TREN**	**BARCO**

Make sure you call out the word when you find it:

```
B  A  O  T  A  M  B  O  R  O  P
J  U  E  G  O  E  B  S  T  B  A
B  U  A  G  E  O  I  A  L  A  T
O  G  E  L  L  P  C  L  T  T  I
C  U  S  G  L  A  I  C  I  E  N
R  A  T  I  O  J  C  G  P  A  E
A  N  E  R  T  U  L  O  A  N  T
B  T  R  E  A  P  E  L  O  T  A
O  E  E  G  U  A  T  O  E  A  D
G  L  O  B  O  D  A  D  L  O  S
```

To talk about more than one thing in SPANISH, change the *el* to *los* . . .

the friend
el amigo

the friend**s**
*los amigo**s***

. . . and the *la* to *las* . . .

the lamp
la lámpara

the lamp**s**
*las lámpara**s***

Try some, and then check your answers:

the toy   *el juguete*

the toys   _____

the skateboard   *la patineta*

the skateboards   _____

ANSWERS: *los juguetes, las patinetas*

29

Now let's count a few toys together. How many do you see?

tres guantes

_____

_____

_____

Los animales de peluche
(Stuffed Animals)

Don't forget your favorite stuffed animals! Say their names slowly:

elephant	*el elefante*
lion	*el león*
rabbit	*el conejo*
tiger	*el tigre*

giraffe *la jirafa*

puppy *el perrito*

dinosaur *el dinosaurio*

The Awesome Word *ES*

The word **es** means "It's." Think of the thousands of sentences you can make in SPANISH with it!

It's the tiger.	***Es el tigre.***
It's the elephant.	***Es el*** _____ .
It's the rabbit.	***Es*** _____ .
It's the lion.	_____ .
It's the teddy bear.	_____ .

Did You Say "My" *(mi)* or "Your" *(tu)*?

Practice saying "my" and "your" in SPANISH:

It's <u>my</u> elephant.   ***Es <u>mi</u> elefante.***
It's <u>your</u> giraffe.   ***Es <u>tu</u> jirafa.***

It's <u>my</u> tiger.   ***Es <u>mi</u> tigre.***
It's <u>your</u> lion.   ***Es <u>tu</u> león.***

It's <u>my</u> teddy bear.   ***Es <u>mi</u> osito.***
It's <u>your</u> puppy.   ***Es <u>tu</u> perrito.***

teddy bear   ***el osito***

Read these SPANISH words aloud and then write what they mean:

mi elefante   <u>my elephant</u>

catorce perritos   _____

los tigres   _____

tu jirafa   _____

dieciséis ositos   _____

ANSWERS: fourteen puppies, the tigers, your giraffe, sixteen teddy bears

¡Dime!
(Tell me!)

Tell your friends and family to do something in SPANISH, and soon, they will learn it, too! Start in the bedroom. Call Mom or Dad, and tell her or him in SPANISH what to do! If they don't get it at first, show off by explaining it to them:

Touch . . .	*Toca . . .*	*. . . la cama*
		. . . la mesa
Point to . . .	*Señala . . .*	*. . . el libro*
		. . . la puerta
Look at . . .	*Mira . . .*	*. . . el juguete*
		. . . la silla

Follow these commands!

Toca el libro.
Mira la puerta.
Señala la cama.

Did you touch the book, look at the door, and point to the bed?
¡Muy bien! Now read the words below, and write what they
mean in English:

Toca los tres juguetes. _____

OK, do the same with these words.
But this time, you'll have to read them backwards first!

.satolep sies sal alañeS
Señala las seis pelotas.   <u>Point to the six balls.</u>

.senoel eveun sol ariM

_____   _____ .

.sarapmál sod sal acoT

_____   _____ .

33

Los colores
(The Colors)

Let's learn some colors in SPANISH. Point to things of the same color as you say each word:

blue	*azul*
black	*negro*
yellow	*amarillo*
brown	*café*
purple	*morado*

red *rojo*

green *verde*

white *blanco*

pink *rosado*

orange *anaranjado*

Use this question to practice the colors in SPANISH!

What color is it?
¿De qué color es?

El conejo es _____ .

¿De qué color es?

El _____ .

ANSWERS: *El conejo es blanco.*
El osito es negro.

SPANISH words are put together differently. To say what color something is, put the color <u>after</u> the word instead of before.

Color these pictures as you read the words!

The <u>red</u> ball	*La pelota <u>roja</u>*
The <u>blue</u> truck	*El camión <u>azul</u>*
The <u>brown</u> dog	*El perro <u>café</u>*

Now there are two. Do you see the difference?

The <u>red</u> balls	*Las pelotas <u>rojas</u>*
The <u>blue</u> trucks	*Los camiones <u>azules</u>*
The <u>brown</u> dogs	*Los perros <u>cafés</u>*

Don't worry if you make mistakes when you practice.
You will get a little better every day!

Now, draw lines to connect these words all by yourself!

café	yellow
rosado	purple
blanco	red
azul	brown
anaranjado	black
amarillo	blue
negro	green
verde	white
rojo	orange
morado	pink

ANSWERS: *café* brown | *rosado* pink | *blanco* white | *azul* blue | *anaranjado* orange | *amarillo* yellow | *negro* black | *verde* green | *rojo* red | *morado* purple

Mi ropa
(My Clothes)

Before you leave the bedroom, put on your clothes in SPANISH!
Say these words every day when you need to get dressed:

I put on the . . .	*Me pongo . . .*
I take off the . . .	*Me quito . . .*

t-shirt	*la camiseta*
shirt	*la camisa*
shorts	*los pantalones cortos*
dress	*el vestido*
sweater	*el suéter*
shoes	*los zapatos*

pants *los pantalones*

socks *los calcetines*

skirt *la falda*

jacket *la chaqueta*

belt *el cinturón*

cap *la gorra*

And what do you wear when the weather is bad?

boots	*las botas*
overcoat	*el abrigo*
raincoat	*el impermeable*

What Is *un* and *una*?

This is how you say "a" or "an" in SPANISH.
Use *un* with words that end in *o*:

<u>A</u> shoe	*<u>Un</u> zapato*
<u>An</u> overcoat	*<u>Un</u> abrigo*

And *una* with words that end in *a*:

<u>A</u> cap	*<u>Una</u> gorra*
<u>A</u> skirt	*<u>Una</u> falda*

Read these SPANISH words aloud:

It's a jacket.	*Es una chaqueta.*
I put on a sweater.	*Me pongo un suéter.*
It's a white shirt.	*Es una camisa blanca.*

Put Them Together!

For fun, add the little word *y*, which means "and"
or the word *o*, which means "or":

I put on a white shirt <u>and</u> a red sweater.
Me pongo una camisa blanca <u>y</u> un suéter rojo.

I take off the jacket <u>or</u> the cap.
Me quito la chaqueta <u>o</u> la gorra.

Look how much SPANISH you know!
Can you do this CROSSWORD PUZZLE?

ACROSS
1. socks
3. raincoat
7. pants

DOWN
1. t-shirt
2. sweater
4. boots
5. skirt
6. cap

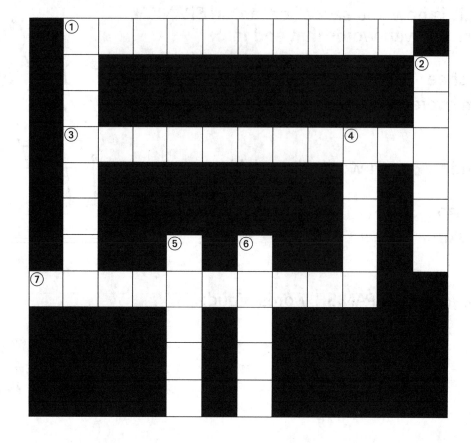

You see—it's easy when
you take the time
to practice.

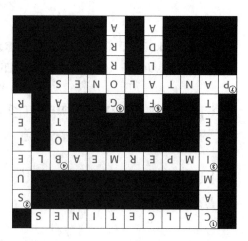

Let's practice what you've learned. Draw lines from the SPANISH sentences to the correct English sentences and read aloud:

Mira los zapatos rojos.	How old are you?
¿Cómo te llamas?	I put on my clothes.
Señala tu juguete.	What color is it?
¿Cuántos años tienes?	Look at the red shoes.
¿Entiendes?	What's happening?
Toca las dos sillas.	Point to your toy.
Es café y azul.	Do you understand?
¿Qué pasa?	It is brown and blue.
Me pongo mi ropa.	Touch the two chairs.
¿De qué color es?	What's your name?

Did you read everything aloud? *¡Muy bien!*

How about a few more clothes?

sandals
las sandalias

bathing suit
el traje de baño

sneakers
las zapatillas

blouse   *la blusa*

suit
el traje

mittens
los mitones

scarf
la bufanda

underwear
la ropa interior

40

3 CHAPTER TRES

En mi casa

(In My Home)

Guillermo,
el padre

María,
la madre

Francisco,
el hijo

Catalina,
la hija

Elena,
la abuela

Rubén,
el abuelo

La familia
(The Family)

Who do you see first in the morning?
Say **Buenos días** to these people every day:

mother **madre**
wife **esposa**

María,
la madre

father **padre**
husband **esposo**

Guillermo,
el padre

brother **hermano**
son **hijo**

Francisco,
el hijo

sister **hermana**
daughter **hija**

Catalina,
la hija

grandmother
abuela

Elena,
la abuela

grandfather
abuelo

Rubén,
el abuelo

Want to learn some more?

uncle **tío**
aunt **tía**
cousin **primo**

It's easy to talk about the family:

Linda es mi hermana. Linda is my sister.
Víctor es mi padre. Victor is my father.
Laura es mi tía. Laura is my aunt.

Now write the names of your family members:

_____ *es mi madre.*

_____ *es mi* _____ .

_____ .

Ask someone in your *familia* to practice SPANISH with you.
You read #1 while the other person reads #2:

#1: *Hola,* (the person's name).
#2: *Buenos días,* (your name).
#1: *¿Cómo estás?*
#2: *Bien, ¿y tú?*
#1: *Muy bien, gracias.*

One way to learn these words is to look at pictures of your family
and follow these commands:

	madre
Señala tu . . .	*hermano*
Mira tu . . .	*padre*
Toca tu . . .	*abuelo*
	hermana

To say "his" or "her" in SPANISH, use the little word *su*:

Linda es <u>su</u> hermana.   Linda is <u>his</u> sister.
Víctor es <u>su</u> padre.   Victor is <u>her</u> father.

¿Quién?
(Who?)

Look at the family on page 42, and then answer the questions below:

¿Quién es el padre?   _____

¿Quién es la hija?   _____

¿Quién es el hijo?   _____

ANSWERS: *Guillermo, Catalina, Francisco*

¡Muy bien! Now answer these questions about <u>your</u> family:

   ¿Cómo se llama tu padre?   _____

   ¿Quién es tu madre?   _____

   ¿Cómo está tu familia?   _____

Underline every other letter to find out the secret message.
The first one is done for you:

a <u>m</u> o i s f t a b m u i r l m i n a e e l s o m d u a y l g o r s a t n a d r e .

ANSWER: *Mi familia es muy grande.*

44

¡Qué bonita!
(How pretty!)

What do the people in your family look like?
Say a few things about them as you move
through the house:

Es…
(He is… or She is…)

pretty   *bonito*
young   *joven*
good   *bueno*
ugly   *feo*
bad   *malo*
small   *chico*

big *grande*

strong *fuerte*

tall *alto*

thin *delgado*

old *viejo*

short *bajo*

fat *gordo*

weak *débil*

Don't forget to change the final *o* to *a* when you talk about girls and
women! What do these words mean in English?

Mi padre es bajo y gordo,
y mi madre es alta, delgada y bonita.

ANSWER: My father is short and fat, and my mother is tall, thin, and pretty.

Connect the opposites!

blanco	*grande*
mucho	*bueno*
madre	*negro*
viejo	*adiós*
chico	*joven*
hola	*padre*
malo	*poco*

Here are some more SPANISH words that describe. If you learn them by heart, think how much you'll be able to say in SPANISH!

The man is . . .   *El hombre es . . .*

nice	*simpático*
handsome	*guapo*
funny	*chistoso*
brave	*valiente*
smart	*inteligente*

Add *muy*, which means "very."
El hombre es muy valiente.

46

Put different names next to the words below. Think of famous people, friends, or even someone who lives in your house!

¡ _____ es muy bonita!

¡ _____ es muy valiente!

¡ _____ es muy chistosa!

¡ _____ es muy guapo!

¡ _____ es muy inteligente!

¡ _____ es muy fuerte!

Add the word *¡Qué...!* if you want to show surprise.
Write the English as you speak out loud:

¡Qué bonito!

How <u>pretty</u>!

¡Qué feo!

How _____ !

¡Qué chistoso!

How _____ !

¡Qué valiente!

How _____ !

ANSWERS: How ugly! How funny! How brave!

47

Él y ella
(He and She)

Let's learn how to say "he" and "she" in SPANISH.
Read all these words aloud:

John is my brother.   *Juan es mi hermano.*
He is small.   *<u>Él</u> es chico.*
He is very young.   *<u>Él</u> es muy joven.*

Mary is my sister.   *María es my hermana.*
She is funny.   *<u>Ella</u> es chistosa.*
She is very smart.   *<u>Ella</u> es muy inteligente.*

Put *Él* or *Ella* in place of the names below. The first one shows you how:

¿Dónde está <u>Sr. Smith</u>?   <u>él</u>

Mira a <u>Laura</u>.   _____

<u>Alicia</u> es una niña bonita.   _____

<u>David</u> es un hombre fuerte.   _____

¿Cómo está <u>Gloria</u>?   _____

ANSWERS: *ella, Él, ella, ella*

48

Más de uno
(More Than One)

If you want to describe more than one person or thing in SPANISH, use the word **son** instead of **es:**

He's big.
Es grande.

They are big.
Son grandes.

He's small.
Es chico.

They are small.
Son chicos.

Be sure to add ***s*** to the word that describes:

The man is tall.
El hombre es alto.

The men are tall.
Los hombres son altos.

Can you understand what these words mean?

Mis amigos son fuertes.   _____ .

Tus abuelos son viejos.   _____ .

Las niñas son inteligentes.   _____ .

This time, talk about many instead of only one:

Mi hermana es bonita.   <u>**Mis hermanas son bonitas.**</u>

Mi hermano es bueno.   _____.

Mi amiga es simpática.   _____.

ANSWERS: *Mis hermanos son buenos.*
Mis amigas son simpáticas.

So, when you describe, don't forget to add *s* when you talk of many things or people.

The <u>tall</u> man.	**El hombre <u>alto</u>.**
The <u>tall</u> men.	**Los hombres <u>altos</u>.**

Tú y yo
(You and I)

Let's learn how to say "you" and "I" in SPANISH.

Tú (You)

Yo (I)

Use the word *Quién* (Who) to practice.
We learned all of these words earlier:

¿Quién es delgado? __Yo__
(Who is thin?)

¿Quién es gordo? __Tú__
(Who is fat?)

¿Quién es muy, muy inteligente?
(Who is very, very smart?)

_____

Connect the SPANISH word with its meaning:

Ella	He
Yo	You
Él	I
Tú	She

51

Bienvenidos a mi casa
(Welcome to My Home)

After you speak SPANISH to your family, go around the house and name everything you see. And don't forget the words you learned in Chapter Two (*En mi cuarto*).

attic
el desván

bedroom
el dormitorio

bathroom
el baño

curtain
la cortina

lights
las luces

garage
el garaje

living room
la sala

rug
la alfombra

stairs
la escalera

dining room
el comedor

cabinet
el gabinete

kitchen
la cocina

Follow this new command!

Let's go to the . . .

Vamos a . . .

Let's go to the living room.

Vamos a la sala.

Let's go to the kitchen.

Vamos a _____.

Let's go to the stairs.

_____.

Cross out the one word that doesn't belong with the others:

la ventana, la jirafa, las cortinas

el carro, el garaje, el hermano

el juguete, la cocina, el comedor

la lámpara, las luces, la falda

el libro, el piso, el techo

¿Dónde está?
(Where is it?)

Use the word *está* to tell where something or someone is.

The book is on the table.
El libro está en la mesa.

My father is in his room.
Mi padre está en su cuarto.

Fill in the word *está* and write what the words mean in English:

Tony <u>está</u> en el comedor.   <u>Tony is in the dining room.</u>

Mi hermana _____ en el garaje.   _____.

El baño _____ en la casa.   _____.

La muñeca _____ en el piso.   _____.

Tu camisa _____ en el dormitorio.   _____.

Use *están* when you are talking about more than one person or thing:

Where <u>are they</u>?
¿Dónde <u>están</u>?

<u>They are</u> in the bathroom.
<u>Están</u> en el baño.

Guess where the girls are hiding:

¿Dónde están las niñas?   ¡Están en el garaje!

Más cosas en la casa
(More Things in the House)

Move from room to room, learning the names for everything in SPANISH. Write these words on little sticky notes. Then, stick them on the furniture so you won't forget.

couch   *el sofá*
refrigerator   *el refrigerador*
dryer   *la secadora*
trash can   *el bote de basura*

desk *el escritorio*

armchair *el sillón*

stove *la estufa*

television *el televisor*

washer *la lavadora*

54

Connect the English words with their meaning in SPANISH:

The washer is white.	*El sillón es bonito.*
Where is the stove?	*¿Dónde están las sillas?*
Your couch is in the house.	*¿Dónde está la estufa?*
My desk is brown.	*La lavadora es blanca.*
The armchair is pretty.	*Mi escritorio es café.*
Where are the chairs?	*Tu sofá está en la casa.*

Now unscramble these letters and write what the words mean in English:

ESPAÑOL	ENGLISH
la raavload	_____
el veroteils	_____
la fuetas	_____

Ellos y ellas
(They [Boys] and They [Girls])

When you say "they" referring to boys, men, and all the male animals, birds (and even fish!) you say *ellos*. And when you say "they" referring to girls, women, and all the female animals (and also fish!) you say *ellas*.

They are bulls.	***El<u>los</u> son tor<u>os</u>.***
They are boys.	***El<u>los</u> son niñ<u>os</u>.***
They are cows.	***Ell<u>as</u> son vac<u>as</u>.***
They are women.	***Ell<u>as</u> son señor<u>as</u>.***

Did you see the *as* and *os* endings?
Did you see how they match?

Aquí y allí
(Here and There)

"EN" means "IN"
"EN" means "ON"
"EN" means "AT"

Sometimes things in the house get moved around. These next SPANISH words will help you find what you're looking for.

Start with the word *en*, which can mean "in," "at," or "on":

Mi madre está en la cocina, en la mesa, en la silla.
My mom is <u>in</u> the kitchen, <u>at</u> the table, <u>on</u> the chair.

And look at these! (Keep reading aloud!)

up	*arriba*	behind	*detrás*
inside	*adentro*		
in front	*enfrente*		
outside	*afuera*		

near *cerca*

under *bajo*

down *abajo*

above *encima*

far *lejos*

Finish these sentences with any of the words above:

It's _____ .   *Está* _____ .

They're _____ .   *Están* _____ .

Look at this picture. Write these words inside the balloons below.

detrás   *adentro*   *enfrente*   *afuera*

Where are they—*arriba* or *abajo*?

el piso   _____

las luces   _____

la alfombra   _____

el techo   _____

58

¿Cómo es?
(What does it look like?)

Use these words to describe the things in your *casa:*

full   *lleno*
expensive   *caro*
cheap   *barato*
empty   *vacío*

cold *frío*

new *nuevo*

hot *caliente*

clean *limpio*

old *vieja*

dirty *sucio*

Read every word aloud!

El sillón es nuevo.	The armchair is new.
Las cortinas están limpias.	The curtains are clean.
La estufa está caliente.	The stove is hot.

¡Muy bien! Now finish these with the missing word:

It's dirty.   *Está* _____ .

It's full.   *Está* _____ .

It's cold.   *Está* _____ .

¿O o A?
(O or A?)

When you talk about a thing that ends in **o**, the word that describes it usually does too. Look:

El zapato es negr_o_ y bonit_o_.
The shoe is black and pretty.

See? The name of the thing is **zapato**, so what we say about it should end in **o** (**negr_o_, bonit_o_**).

Also, if the name of the thing ends in **a**, then what we say about it often ends in **a**. Look:

La silla es negr_a_ y bonit_a_.
The chair is black and pretty.

Let's see if you got it. Add **o** or **a** to the words that describe.

1. **La sill_a_ es barat__ y limpi__ .**

2. **El tech_o_ es blanc__ y bonit__ .**

3. **La alfombr_a_ es roj__ y morad__ .**

4. **La lámpar_a_ es fe__ y chic__ .**

5. **El librer_o_ es baj__ y viej__ .**

Now connect the opposites:

enfrente	**caro**
arriba	**lejos**
frío	**ella**
afuera	**allí**
él	**adentro**
cerca	**caliente**
barato	**detrás**
aquí	**abajo**

ANSWERS:

enfrente	detrás
arriba	abajo
frío	caliente
afuera	adentro
él	ella
cerca	lejos
barato	caro
aquí	allí

No! No! No!
(Not! Not! Not!)

Use **No** to say "NOT" in SPANISH. Watch:

It's clean.	**Está limpio.**
It's <u>not</u> clean.	**<u>No</u> está limpio.**
They're old.	**Son viejos.**
They're <u>not</u> old.	**<u>No</u> son viejos.**

You try one. Fill in the missing words:

My book is here.	**<u>Mi libro está aquí.</u>**
My book is not here.	_____

ANSWERS: *Mi libro no está aquí.*

Keep speaking SPANISH around the house. Can you guess what these words mean?

Mi familia está en la casa. La casa es blanca, azul, y grande. El garaje está enfrente de la casa. La familia no está en el garaje. Mi padre y mi madre están en la cocina. Ellos están cerca de la estufa y el refrigerador. Mis dos hermanos están en la sala. Son muy chistosos. Están enfrente del televisor. ¿Dónde está tu familia y cómo es tu casa?

These three questions are great for talking about your *casa*.
Go ahead—answer everything in *ESPAÑOL*:

Where do you live?   I live in _____ .

¿Dónde vives?   *Vivo en _____ .*

What's your address?   My address is _____ .

¿Cuál es tu dirección?   *Mi dirección es _____ .*

_____

_____

What's your phone number?   My number is _____ .

¿Cuál es tu número de teléfono?   *Mi número es _____ .*

But we're not finished yet!
Let's go to another part of the house
to learn more SPANISH every day . . .

Here are more words that you can use to make whole sentences:

basement	*el sótano*
hallway	*el pasillo*
chimney	*la chimenea*
fireplace	*el fogón*
porch	*el porche*
roof	*el tejado*
yard	*el patio*
stool	*el banquillo*
nightstand	*la mesita de noche*
chest	*el baúl*

CHAPTER *CUATRO*

A la cocina

(To the Kitchen)

grapes
las uvas

milk
la leche

watermelon
la sandía

eggs
los huevos

strawberries
las fresas

sodas
los refrescos

ham
el jamón

fish
el pescado

oranges
las naranjas

butter
la mantequilla

juice
el jugo

cheese
el queso

meat
la carne

bread
el pan

¿Cómo estás?
(How are you?)

On your way to the kitchen, find out how everyone is feeling today:

I am . . .   *Estoy . . .*

fine *bien*

happy *feliz*

excited *emocionado*

Sometimes, we don't feel very well. Put in any word that fits:

Are you . . . ?   *¿Estás . . . ?*

sad *triste*

angry *enojada*

tired *cansada*

Use the words *estoy* and *estás* to talk about how you feel
and where you are.

Where are you?   *¿Dónde estás?*

I'm in the kitchen.   *Estoy en la cocina.*

Ask someone to read along with you.
Each person takes a different part:

#1 *¿Cómo estás?*
#2 *Estoy muy feliz, gracias.*
   Mis amigos están en mi casa.
   ¿Y tú?
#1 *Estoy muy triste.*
   Mis amigos no están bien.
#2 *¿Dónde están tus amigos?*
#1 *No están aquí. ¡Están en la cama!*

Do you know what you are saying?

ANSWERS:
#1 How are you?
#2 I'm very happy, thanks. My friends are at my house.
And you?
#1 I'm very sad. My friends are not well.
#2 Where are your friends?
#1 They're not here. They're in bed!

Connect with lines the right picture with the right word:

cansada   *enojada*   *feliz*

66

Tengo mucha hambre
(I'm very hungry)

Does speaking SPANISH make you hungry? Go into the kitchen and find something to eat:

El desayuno
(Breakfast)

egg **el huevo**

bread **el pan**

cheese **el queso**

fruit **la fruta**

meat **la carne**

milk **la leche**

butter **la mantequilla**

juice **el jugo**

Use these new words EVERY DAY. Put anything you like on the left-hand lines below, and then see if you can write it in SPANISH on the right-hand ones:

Do you like _____ ?   ☞   *¿Te gusta _____ ?*

Yes, I like _____ .   ☞   *Sí, me gusta _____ .*

Do you want _____ ?   ☞   *¿Quieres _____ ?*

Yes, I want _____ .   ☞   *Sí, quiero _____ .*

Let's practice what we learned at breakfast. Fill in all the missing letters:

p __ n   __ ues __   __ ar __ e

h __ __ vo   __ r __ t __   __ ug __

¿Te gusta la fruta? Do you like fruit? Which one is your favorite?

My favorite fruit is …   *Mi fruta favorita es …*

 strawberry *la fresa*

 banana *el plátano*

 apple *la manzana*

 orange *la naranja*

 grape *la uva*

watermelon *la sandía*

Be sure to add <u>color</u> to all these pictures!

Which one is bigger? Underline your answer:

la naranja o la uva

la manzana o la sandía

el plátano o la fresa

Esto y eso
(This and That)

Test yourself! Touch something and say:

What is <u>this</u>?   *¿Qué es <u>esto</u>?*

Then, point to something else and ask:

What is <u>that</u>?   *¿Qué es <u>eso</u>?*

Los vegetales
(Vegetables)

Open the refrigerator and look for any vegetables.
Take out each one as you practice aloud:
¿Qué es esto? Es . . .

potato *la papa*

onion *la cebolla*

tomato *el tomate*

lettuce *la lechuga*

corn *el maíz*

carrot *la zanahoria*

celery *el apio*

beans *los frijoles*

You have a lot of words to remember. Connect the sentences that mean the same:

Me gusta la sandía.	The celery is thin.
Mira el pan blanco.	The juice is cold.
Las uvas son buenas.	I want my breakfast.
La papa es grande.	I like the watermelon.
Las naranjas están aquí.	The butter is there.
Los huevos son chicos.	Look at the white bread.
El jugo está frío.	The oranges are here.
La mantequilla está allí.	The grapes are good.
El apio es delgado.	The eggs are small.
Yo quiero mi desayuno.	The potato is big.

This time, connect each food with its color:

la fresa	anaranjada
la lechuga	blanca
el plátano	roja
la zanahoria	amarillo
la leche	verde

You will not go far if you don't know how to ask "How many?"
and "How much?"

How many?   *¿Cuántos?*

     ¿Cuántos plátanos?   *¿Dos o tres?*
¡Tres!

How much?   *¿Cuánto?*

¿Cuánta leche?   *¿Mucha o poca?*
¡Mucha!

Más comida
(More Food)

Call out these new commands in the kitchen.

Eat . . .
Come . . .

Take . . .   *Toma . . .*

Bring . . .
Trae . . .

El almuerzo
(Lunch)

hamburger *la hamburguesa*   hot dog *el perro caliente*
salad *la ensalada*
soup *la sopa*   french fries *las papas fritas*

sandwich *el sandwich*

La cena
(Dinner)

chicken *el pollo*
ham *el jamón*

turkey *el pavo*

fish *el pescado*

steak *el bistec*

Cross out the one word that doesn't belong with the other two:

leche, jugo, jamón

piso, pavo, pollo

lechuga, tomate, juguete

pescado, desayuno, almuerzo

manzana, camisa, naranja

toma, come, apio

ANSWERS: *jamón, piso, juguete, pescado, camisa, apio*

Choose the best word to finish the phrase:

ensalada   mantequilla   naranja

pan y _____

jugo de _____

sopa y _____

ANSWERS:
mantequilla
naranja
ensalada

Practice saying these with a friend today:

¡Qué sabroso!
How tasty!

¿Tienes hambre?   **Sí, tengo mucha hambre.**
Are you hungry?   Yes, I'm very hungry.

¿Tienes sed?   **Sí, tengo mucha sed.**
Are you thirsty?   Yes, I'm very thirsty.

Las bebidas
(Drinks)

Ask your family in SPANISH! Use these questions:

Do you like . . .   **¿Te gusta . . . ?**
Do you want . . .   **¿Quieres . . . ?**

lemonade *la limonada*
milk shake *el batido*
hot chocolate *el chocolate caliente*

tea *el té*   soda *el refresco*

Which do you like better? Circle your answer:

el agua o el batido

la leche o el refresco

el chocolate caliente o el té

Write three words under each category:

Los vegetales	_Las frutas_	_Las bebidas_
_____	_____	_____
_____	_____	_____
_____	_____	_____

Find these words in the WORD SEARCH puzzle below:

CARNE   PAN   LECHE   HUEVO   MANZANA   UVA

FRESA   TOMATE   PAVO   SOPA   APIO   REFRESCO

```
O   E   C   S   O   P   A   H   U   S
A   H   O   T   O   V   A   P   I   O
R   C   O   A   E   T   A   M   O   T
E   E   P   A   C   T   T   P   F   A
F   L   E   N   A   P   I   E   R   N
R   P   R   V   R   Z   H   A   E   A
E   F   O   T   N   C   A   P   S   Z
S   A   H   U   E   V   O   F   A   N
C   S   V   L   P   A   R   U   V   A
O   U   A   A   R   E   T   T   O   M
```

Here's another dialogue to practice:

#1 *¿Tienes hambre?*

#2 *Sí, tengo mucha hambre.*
   Vamos a la cocina.

#1 *Muy bien.*
   ¿Te gusta la fruta?

#2 *Sí, quiero las uvas, por favor.*

#1 *¿Cuántas quieres?*

#2 *¡Muchas!*

#2 A lot!
#1 How many do you want?
#2 Yes, I want grapes, please.
#1 Great. Do you like fruit?
#2 Yes, I'm very hungry. Let's go to the kitchen.
#1 Are you hungry?
ANSWERS:

Más números
(More Numbers)

It's time to learn more numbers, so let's practice these words right now. First, count from one to twenty in SPANISH as fast as you can:

1, 2, 3, 4, 5, 6, 7, 8, 9, 10, 11, 12, 13, 14, 15, 16, 17, 18, 19, 20

¡Fantástico! To say 21, just put 20 and 1 together:

veinte   y   uno

Can you finish this list all by yourself?

22 _____ 24 _____

23 _____ 25 _____

Here are other numbers you should know:

30	*treinta*	40	*cuarenta*
50	*cincuenta*	60	*sesenta*
70	*setenta*	80	*ochenta*
90	*noventa*	100	*cien*

And what about all the numbers in between?

31 *treinta y uno* 55 *cincuenta y cinco*

72 _____ 99 _____

Practice your numbers in SPANISH every day:

Find out the ages of everyone in your *familia*.

Count all the toys, books, or shoes in the *casa*.

Read every page number in this book in *español*.

¿Qué hora es?
(What time is it?)

After you eat, check the kitchen clock. It's easy to tell time in SPANISH. Just say the hour . . .

It's three o'clock.
Son las tres.

It's eight o'clock.
Son las ocho.

. . . and then add the minutes:

It's 3:10.
Son las tres y diez.

It's 7:45.
Son las siete y cuarenta y cinco.

O.K. Connect each clock with the correct time:

Son las cuatro y quince.

Es la una.

Son las doce.

Son las siete y cuarenta y cinco.

Es la una y treinta.

This is how you say "at" a certain time:

<u>At</u> 2:00
***A las* dos**

<u>At</u> 9:20
***A las* nueve y veinte**

<u>At</u> 5:05
***A las* cinco y cinco**

Answer these questions *en español* :

When do you go to bed?   ***A las* _____** .

When do you go to school? ***A las* _____** .

When do you wake up?   ***A las* _____** .

¿Qué día es hoy?
(What day is today?)

After you give the time in SPANISH, tell everyone what day it is.
Use the kitchen calendar:

Today is . . .
Hoy es . . .

1	2	3	4	5	6	7
Lunes	Martes	Miércoles	Jueves	Viernes	Sábado	Domingo

These words are spelled backwards. Write them correctly, and then put them in the right order:

seveuj   *senul*   *ognimod*   *setram*

_____   _____   _____   _____

senreiv   *selocréim*   *odabás*

_____   _____   _____

1. _____

2. _____

3. _____

4. _____

5. _____

6. _____

7. _____

79

¿Cuál es la fecha?
(What's the date?)

Learn these months and you will be able to say today's date in a different language!

January *enero*
February *febrero*
March *marzo*

July *julio*
August *agosto*
September *septiembre*

April *abril*
May *mayo*
June *junio*

October *octubre*
November *noviembre*
December *diciembre*

Be careful! In SPANISH, the number goes first:

Oct. 5th   el *cinco* de octubre
May 21st   el *veinte y uno* de mayo
Dec. 12th   el *doce* de diciembre

Learn these words, too:

week *la semana*   month *el mes*   year *el año*

Say in SPANISH:

June 15th

Sept. 30th

March 22nd

80

Translate, and then answer the question:

¿Cuántos días en una semana? _____

¿Cuántos meses en un año? _____

Go look at the clock and calendar right now:

¿Qué hora es? _____

¿Qué día es hoy? _____

¿Cuál es la fecha? _____

¿Cuándo?
(When?)

¿Cuándo?

Choose any of these words to talk about time:

today	*hoy*
tomorrow	*mañana*
yesterday	*ayer*
always	*siempre*
never	*nunca*
sometimes	*a veces*

12:00

Many SPANISH words can be learned in pairs:

before	*antes*	after	*después*
early	*temprano*	late	*tarde*

81

Ready to practice? Connect the opposites:

antes   **siempre**
nunca   **temprano**
ayer   **después**
tarde   **hoy**

These two <u>new</u> command words go well with the clock and the calendar:

Come . . .
Ven . . .

Go . . .
Anda . . .

. . . **a las ocho**
. . . **en tres semanas**
. . . **en enero**
. . . **temprano mañana**
. . . **en una hora**
. . . **antes de las cuatro**
. . . **en dos meses**
. . . **el miércoles**

Use this code to figure out the secret day of the year!

1	2	3	4	5	6	7	8	9	10	11	12	13	14	15	16	17	18	19	20	21	22	23	24	25
A	B	C	D	E	F	G	H	I	J	K	L	M	N	O	P	Q	R	S	T	U	V	W	X	Y

5-12   22-5-9-14-20-5   25   3-9-14-3-15   4-5   4-9-3-9-5-13-2-18-5

82

Before we leave this chapter, check these fruits and vegetables.
How many can you remember with just one glance?

rice	*el arroz*
noodle	*el fideo*
green bean	*la judía verde*
pea	*la arvejita*
pumpkin	*la calabaza*
lemon	*el limón*
peach	*el melocotón*
pear	*la pera*

The kitchen is full of SPANISH, but there is still more to come.
If you want, read CHAPTER *CUATRO* one more time before moving ahead.
And don't forget—keep speaking SPANISH every day!

5 CHAPTER
CINCO

Vamos afuera

(Let's Go Outside)

¿Qué tiempo hace?
(How's the weather?)

It's time to learn SPANISH outside the house. Start by saying something about the weather:

It's . . .   *Está . . .*

raining **lloviendo**
windy **ventoso**

cloudy **nublado**

snowing **nevando**

You can also use the word *Hace:*

It's . . .   *Hace . . .*

cold   *frío*
sunny   *sol*
hot   *calor*

Now, connect the words that mean the same:

It's snowing.   **Hace sol.**
It's sunny.   **Está lloviendo.**
It's raining.   **Está nevando.**

Draw this picture:

Es un día bonito. No está nublado. Hace mucho sol.

Look outside right now and say what you see:

Hace . . .   *Está . . .*

El jardín
(The Garden)

Do you have a garden? Then go outside and walk around. You don't have one? Then imagine it!

Look at the . . .   *Mira . . .*

tree
el árbol

bush
el arbusto

flower
la flor

grass
el pasto

plant
la planta

insect
el insecto

What else do you see or imagine?

dirt *la tierra*

leaf *la hoja*

stones *las piedras*

Color all these pictures today!

The little SPANISH word *Hay* means "There is" or "There are."
It sounds like the word "I" in English:

There is a lot of dirt.   *Hay mucha tierra.*
There are a lot of stones.   *Hay muchas piedras.*

Put these words in order:

There is a lot of grass in the garden:

en   mucho   Hay   el jardín   pasto

_____

There are a lot of leaves on the bush:

el arbusto   hojas   Hay   en   muchas

_____

There are bugs and small animals in every garden. Point and speak:

Point to the. . .   *Señala . . .*

ant *la hormiga*

worm *el gusano*

bee *la abeja*

fly *la mosca*

snail *el caracol*

cockroach
la cucaracha

spider *la araña*

Underline the word that doesn't fit:

calor, frío, palo
viento, mosca, abeja
arbusto, tiempo, árbol

Circle the correct answer:

Las hormigas son (*cocinas, calcetines, chicas*)
La flor es (*tierra, pelota, amarilla*)
Hace frío y está (*mesa, lloviendo, arbusto*)

Los animales domésticos
(House Pets)

Do you have pets around the house? Do your friends have any?
Look how different they are in SPANISH:

mouse *el ratón*

dog *el perro*

cat *el gato*

turtle *la tortuga*

bird *el pájaro*

fish *el pez*

Children who live on a farm play with these:

pig *el puerco*

horse *el caballo*

sheep *la oveja*

cow *la vaca*

duck *el pato*

89

Draw a line from each picture to the correct word:

la oveja   *el gato*   *el caballo*   *el pájaro*   *el perro*

Follow this maze through the garden.
Be sure you speak SPANISH along the way!

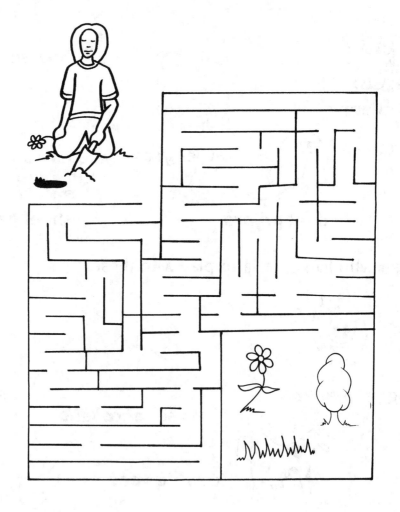

Trabajo en el jardín
(I work in the garden.)

When you go to a garden, these commands will show
how much you know:

Point to the . . .	Señala . . .
Look at the . . .	Mira . . .
Touch the . . .	Toca . . .
Bring the . . .	Trae . . .
Take the . . .	Toma . . .

shovel *la pala*

broom *la escoba*

rake *el rastrillo*

hose *la manguera*

ladder *la escalera*

Más herramientas
(More Tools)

Now, try this command with your tools:

Use the . . . *Use . . .*

pliers *las pinzas*
nail *el clavo*

hammer *el martillo*

saw *el serrucho*

screwdriver *el destornillador*

Are you still coloring? Circle the word that fits the sentence:

(La escalera, la flor, la oveja) es un animal.

(El serrucho, la tortuga, el árbol) es una herramienta.

(El rastrillo, el arbusto, la vaca) es una planta.

Now, connect the words that belong together:

las hojas	*el martillo*
la tierra	*la escoba*
el piso	*el rastrillo*
el clavo	*la manguera*
el agua	*la pala*

Cross out every other letter and read the secret message:

M o e t g o u p s í t r a s m ó i f j m a n r e d o í o n a .

¡Vamos!
(Let's go!)

When you are finished in the garden, ask someone to give you a ride around town. SPANISH is everywhere, so get ready to learn a lot.

I like the . . . *Me gusta . . .*

car   *el carro*
subway   *el metro*

truck   *el camión*

motorcycle   *la motocicleta*

bus   *el autobús*

Choose the best word from the list above:

Students take this to school.   _____

Only one police officer can ride on it.   _____

This thing goes underground.   _____

ANSWERS: *el autobús, la motocicleta, el metro*

Which one is bigger?

el camión o la motocicleta
el carro o el metro
el autobús o la bicicleta

ANSWERS: *el camión, el metro, el autobús*

These can carry people, too:

helicopter   *el helicóptero*
boat   *el bote*
train   *el tren*

ship
el barco

plane
el avión

Fill in the missing letters, and then write the English:

e l   _ a _ _ o

_____

l a   _ o t _ _ _ i c _ _ _ t a

_____

e l   _ u _ o b _ s

_____

e l   t _ e _

_____

e l   a _ i _ n

_____

e l   _ _ _ t r _

_____

94

Now, connect the sentences that mean the same:

Vamos en el barco.   Bring the new car.

Los botes son amarillos.   They are on the train.

Trae el carro nuevo.   I like the truck.

Me gusta el camión.   Let's go in the ship.

Están en el tren.   The boats are yellow.

Can you ask these questions in SPANISH?

Where is the car?
What color is the car?
Do you like the car?

La ciudad
(The City)

Look out the window as you go downtown.
When you see something, say it loud in SPANISH:

street	*la calle*
sidewalk	*la acera*
mailbox	*el buzón*

building *el edificio*

traffic light
el semáforo

fence *la cerca*

sign *el letrero*

bridge *el puente*

Keep pointing:

Point to the . . . *Señala . . .*

bank	*el banco*
church	*la iglesia*
school	*la escuela*

restaurant *el restaurante*

store *la tienda*

gas station *la gasolinera*

O.K. Answer these questions in SPANISH:

Where do people keep their money?   *En el banco*

Where do people buy their clothing?   _____

Where do people go out to eat?   _____

Where do people get gas for their cars?   _____

What do these sentences mean?

Vamos al buzón.   _____ .

Vamos a la iglesia.   _____ .

Vamos al puente.   _____ .

A EL = AL
DE EL = DEL

Al y Del
("To the" and "Of the")

Spanish people got tired of saying *a el* and *de el* so they shortened them to *al* and *del*. Look:

Let's go <u>to the</u> mailbox.   *Vamos <u>al</u> buzón.*
It's in front <u>of the</u> building.   *Está enfrente <u>del</u> edificio.*

If you visit the city, use words that tell "where."
Put any of these on the lines below:

detrás   *cerca*   *enfrente*   *lejos*

El letrero está _____ *del restaurante.*

La cerca está _____ *de la escuela.*

El semáforo está _____ *de la calle.*

Connect each picture below with the correct word.
Then, add <u>color</u> to everything!

la flor   *el semáforo*   *el pájaro*   *el edificio*   *el puente*

La gente
(People)

The city is a busy place. Wave to each person you see:

nurse *el enfermero*
firefighter *el bombero*
mechanic *el mecánico*
salesperson *el vendedor*

student *el estudiante*

teacher
el maestro

doctor *el doctor*

police officer *el policía*

Don't forget! Most words that describe girls end in the letter *a*:

*María es una mecánica y
Susana es una enfermera.*
Mary is a mechanic and Susan is a nurse.

Read this story aloud. What does it mean in English?

Mi madre es una doctora. Ella es muy inteligente. No está en la casa hoy. Está en el hospital. Mi padre es un vendedor y es muy chistoso. Es un vendedor de zapatos. No está en su tienda hoy. Él está en la casa.

ANSWER: My mother is a doctor. She is very smart. She is not at home today. She is at the hospital. My father is a salesman and he is very funny. He is a shoe salesman. He is not at his store today. He is at home.

Cross out the word that does not fit:

tienda, banco, restaurante, buzón

caballo, metro, vaca, oveja

vendedor, maestro, martillo, bombero

mecánico, avión, barco, autobús

semáforo, calle, edificio, piedra

ANSWERS: *buzón, metro, martillo, mecánico, piedra*

Más trabajadores
(More Workers)

pilot   *el piloto*
dentist   *el dentista*
secretary   *el secretario*

waiter *el mesero*

mail carrier
la or *el cartero*

cook *el cocinero*

Circle the words that look a lot like English:

el dentista   *el mesero*   *el cartero*   *el doctor*

el bombero   *el piloto*   *el vendedor*   *el cocinero*

ANSWERS: *el dentista, el doctor, el piloto*

Connect the beginning of each sentence with its correct ending:

El cartero está   *en el hospital.*

El piloto está   *en el garaje.*

El cocinero está   *en la calle.*

La doctora está   *en el avión.*

El mecánico está   *en el restaurante.*

Try these questions with friends and their families
who speak only SPANISH:

Do you work?	*¿Trabajas?*
Where do you work?	*¿Dónde trabajas?*
Do you like your job?	*¿Te gusta tu trabajo?*

Write three words under each category:

City Buildings	**Workers**	**Transportation**
_____	_____	_____
_____	_____	_____
_____	_____	_____

¿Quién eres tú?
(Who are you?)

Use the word *Soy* to talk about yourself in SPANISH:

I'm Tina.	*Soy Tina.*
I'm a student.	*Soy estudiante.*
I'm smart.	*Soy inteligente.*

Can you tell what these people are saying?

Soy el Sr. López.   I'm Mr. Lopez.

Soy bombero.   _____ .

Soy muy fuerte.   _____ .

Soy la Sra. González.   I'm Mrs. González.

Soy maestra.   _____ .

Soy de Cuba.   _____ .

Soy Linda.   _____ .

Soy esposa y madre.   _____ .

Soy alta y bonita.   _____ .

ANSWERS: I'm a firefighter. I'm very strong.
I'm a teacher. I'm from Cuba.
I'm Linda. I'm a wife and mother. I'm tall and pretty.

And what about you? *¿Quién eres tú?*

Soy _____ . Soy _____ . Soy _____ .

¡Mira! You can say a lot about yourself in SPANISH.
Read these words aloud:

I'm very happy.	*Soy muy feliz.*
I'm a student of SPANISH.	*Soy estudiante de español.*
I understand a lot of SPANISH.	*Entiendo mucho español.*
I like SPANISH a lot.	*Me gusta mucho el español.*
I want more SPANISH!	*¡Quiero más español!*

Match each question with its answer:

¿Cuándo trabajas?	*Su nombre es Ana.*
¿Eres un maestro?	*Sí, estoy aquí.*
¿Quién es la vendedora?	*Tres.*
¿Estás en la tienda?	*No, soy piloto.*
¿Cuántos policías hay?	*Mañana.*

ANSWERS: *¿Cuándo trabajas?* Mañana.
¿Eres un maestro? No, soy piloto.
¿Quién es la vendedora? Su nombre es Ana.
¿Estás en la tienda? Sí, estoy aquí.
¿Cuántos policías hay? Tres.

Try out this conversation with a friend:

#1 *¿Quién eres tú?*
#2 *Soy policía. ¿Qué quieres?*
#1 *¿Dónde está la tienda de juguetes?*
#2 *Está allí, enfrente del edificio grande.*
#1 *¿Está cerca de la gasolinera?*
#2 *Sí. El letrero es blanco y azul.*
#1 *¡Fantástico! Muchas gracias.*
#2 *De nada. Adiós.*

ANSWERS:
#1 Who are you?
#2 I'm a police officer. What do you want?
#1 Where is the toy store?
#2 It's there, in front of the big building.
#1 Is it near the gas station?
#2 Yes. The sign is white and blue.
#1 Great! Thanks a lot.
#2 You're welcome. Good-bye.

This time, put the letters in numerical order.
Find out where we're going in the next chapter:

M (3)   *L* (7)   *S* (10)   *V* (1)   *A* (15)   *E* (13)   *C* (11)   *A* (6)

O (4)   *A* (2)   *E* (9)   *U* (12)   *A* (8)   *S* (5)   *L* (14)

ANSWER: *Vamos a la escuela.*

Before you finish this chapter, have a look at these places.
They are very important!

crosswalk	*el cruce de peatones*
stop sign	*la señal de parada*
highway	*la carretera*
airport	*el aeropuerto*
factory	*la fábrica*
fire department	*el departamento de bomberos*
supermarket	*el supermercado*
police station	*la estación de policía*
post office	*el correo*
bus stop	*la parada de autobús*

Did you finish all the questions and puzzles in this chapter? *¡Qué bueno!* Now you can turn the page, go to school, and speak more SPANISH every day!

6 CHAPTER
SEIS

En la escuela

(At School)

Mi escuela
(My School)

Speak SPANISH on your way to school. And when you get there, name whatever you see!

Look at the teachers and students.
Mira los maestros y los estudiantes.

Let's go to the . . .	Vamos a . . .
flag	*la bandera*
office	*la oficina*
benches	*los bancos*
classroom	*el salón de clase*
whiteboard	*el pizarrón*
playground	*el campo de recreo*

Study this map. Write the word that matches each number you find:

1. _____

2. _____

3. _____

4. _____

ANSWERS: 1. la bandera 2. la oficina 3. el salón de clase 4. el campo de recreo

Write these "backward" sentences correctly. Then, put what they mean in English:

.anicifo al ed etnerfne átse arednab aL

SPANISH: _____

ENGLISH: _____

.aleucse al ed sárted átse aiselgi aL

SPANISH: _____

ENGLISH: _____

.oercer ed opmac led acrec nátse socnab soL

SPANISH: _____

ENGLISH: _____

ANSWERS:
La bandera está enfrente de la oficina.
The flag is in front of the office.
La iglesia está detrás de la escuela.
The church is behind the school.
Los bancos están cerca del campo de recreo.
The benches are near the playground.

Estoy en el grado cuatro.

Try this question. Just add a number:

What grade are you in?   *¿En qué grado estás?*

I'm in <u>fourth</u> grade.   *Estoy en el grado <u>cuatro</u>.*

Now, remember all the SPANISH words you have learned, and use them to write about yourself:

_____

_____

_____

_____

Mi salón de clase
(My Classroom)

Be very quiet as you practice in the classroom. Look at these things and say their name in SPANISH:

desk *el escritorio*

pencil sharpener
el sacapuntas

bulletin board
el tablero de anuncios

map *el mapa*   bell *la campana*

Unscramble these letters now:

oirtseocri   *tusaacanps*   *maapacn*

_____   _____   _____

Name everything in this backpack. "Backpack" is called *la mochila* in SPANISH.

_____ *está en la mochila.*

paper   *el papel*
pencil   *el lápiz*
pen   *el lapicero*
eraser   *el borrador*
notebook *el cuaderno*

This time, connect each word with its meaning:

pen   *el papel*
pencil   *el cuaderno*
paper   *el lápiz*
desk   *el escritorio*
notebook *el lapicero*

Circle the word that doesn't belong:

el lápiz, el lapicero, el banco

la bandera, la maestra, el estudiante

el papel, la campana, el cuaderno

¿Qué necesitas?
(What do you need?)

Tell everyone what you need in SPANISH:

I need the . . .   *Necesito . . .*

stapler *la engrapadora*

crayons *los gises*

chalk *la tiza*

scissors *las tijeras*

glue *el pegamento*

marker *el marcador*

Connect each picture with the proper word:

las tijeras   los gises   el pegamento   el marcador

Now, fill in the blank with the correct word:

la pelota   el papel   el almuerzo

Tengo hambre. Necesito _____ .

¿Dónde están mis juguetes? Necesito _____ .

Quiero mi cuaderno. Necesito _____ .

You learned these words before, but do you remember them?
Write what they mean in English:

la computadora _____

el reloj _____

el libro _____

el bote de basura _____

el gabinete _____

Put **T** for true and **F** for false:

Los estudiantes están en los escritorios. _____

El pizarrón está en el campo de recreo. _____

Los papeles están en la bandera. _____

El libro está en el salón de clase. _____

Los bancos están en el sacapuntas. _____

The world of communications and computers is your world.
Learn it in Spanish!

cell phone	*el teléfono celular*
e-mail	*el correo electrónico*
keyboard	*el teclado*
laptop	*la computadora portátil*
mouse	*el ratón*
password	*la contraseña*
printer	*la impresora*
screen	*la pantalla*
text message	*el mensaje en texto*
video game	*el videojuego*
website	*el sitio web*

¡Lo tengo!
(I have it!)

Tell others what you have in SPANISH:

Do you have your pencil?	*¿Tienes tu lápiz?*
Yes, I have it!	*¡Sí, lo tengo!*
Do you have your paper?	*¿Tienes tu papel?*
No, I don't have it!	*¡No, no lo tengo!*
Do you have your _____ ?	*¿Tienes tu _____ ?*

The word *tiene* means "has" in SPANISH.

The school <u>has</u> a big office.
La escuela <u>tiene</u> una oficina grande.

The teacher <u>has</u> the scissors and crayons.
El maestro <u>tiene</u> las tijeras y los gises.

My classroom has _____ .

Mi salón de clase tiene _____ .

Put the correct word on the lines below:

tiene   tienes   tengo

¿Tú _____ tu libro?

Yo no _____ mi cuaderno.

Ella _____ su lápiz y borrador.

ANSWERS: *tienes, tengo, tiene*

113

¡*De* es muy necesario!
(*De* is very necessary!)

When something belongs to someone, use the word **de**:

It is Victor's pencil.   **Es el lápiz de Víctor.**

It is the teacher's desk.   **Es el escritorio del maestro.**

Try some:

It's Mary's book.   _____

It's Joe's pen.   _____

ANSWERS: *Es el libro de María.*
Es el lapicero de José.

Mi clase favorita
(My Favorite Class)

You can learn many things at school. What do you like best?

I like . . .   *Me gusta . . .*

I like	Me gusta
music	*la música*
math	*las matemáticas*
art	*el arte*
social studies	*los estudios sociales*
science	*la ciencia*
language	*el lenguaje*

Which of these words go together?

las pinturas	*la ciencia*
los números	*el lenguaje*
el radio	*el arte*
los animales	*las matemáticas*
el español	*la música*

El mundo grande
(The Big World)

Let's learn about the world.

Use a map to practice:

Point to the . . .
Señala . . .

state	*el estado*
country	*el país*
world	*el mundo*

¡Hay muchos países en el mundo!

115

Where do I come from?	¿De dónde vengo?
I come from . . .	Yo vengo de . . .

Canada	*Canadá*
China	*China*
England	*Inglaterra*
France	*Francia*
Germany	*Alemania*
Greece	*Grecia*
Ireland	*Irlanda*
Italy	*Italia*
Japan	*Japón*
Mexico	*México*
Spain	*España*
Switzerland	*Suiza*

Look at the . . .   *Mira* . . .

desert   *el desierto*
lake   *el lago*

forest   *el bosque*

mountain   *la montaña*

river   *el río*

Did you color everything? *¡Muy bien!* Now say where you live:

Vivo en la calle _____ (your street)

Vivo en la ciudad de _____ (your town)

Vivo en el estado de _____ (your state)

Join the words that go together . . .

el desierto   *alta*
la montaña   *azul*
el río   *calor*

. . . and fill in the blank:

botes   *estados*   *árboles*

Hay muchos _____ *en el bosque.*

Hay muchos _____ *en el lago.*

Hay muchos _____ *en el país.*

So, how much SPANISH do you think you know? Let's see! Write what these words mean in English:

Mi país tiene cincuenta estados.   _____

Mira los dos lagos bonitos.   _____

Los tigres están en el bosque.   _____

Hace frío en las montañas.   _____

El desierto está cerca de aquí.   _____

El campo de recreo
(The Playground)

After school, tell the SPANISH names of these fun things:

Let's go to the . . .   *Vamos a . . .*

merry-go-round   *los caballitos*
bars   *las barras*

seesaw   *el subibaja*

swing   *el columpio*

slide   *el resbalador*

Fill in the missing letters:

el __ e __ __ a l __ __ o __   el __ o __ u __ p __ o

el __ __ b i __ a __ __

You learned about these things earlier. Write in the English:

Trae . . .	Bring the . . .
el bate	<u>bat</u>
la pelota	_____
el guante	_____
la bicicleta	_____
la patineta	_____
el juguete	_____

¡Dame!
(Give me!)

Here's a <u>new</u> command. Use **Dame** to say "Give me":

Give me the ball!	**¡Dame la pelota!**
Give me the toy!	_____
Give me the skateboard!	_____

ANSWERS: *¡Dame el juguete!*
¡Dame la patineta!

Los juegos
(The Games)

How do you have fun **en español**?

basketball   **el baloncesto**   soccer **el fútbol**
baseball   **el béisbol**
drawing   **el dibujo**

reading **la lectura**

dancing **el baile**

Put one of these words on the lines below:

I like _____ a lot.   *Me gusta mucho* _____ .

Do you like _____ ?   *¿Te gusta* _____ ?

Match the words that go together:

los gises   *la lectura*
la pelota   *el dibujo*
el libro   *el béisbol*

Put the words in each sentence in the right order:

juego   fútbol   Es   de   un.
dibujo   clase   de   la   Vamos   a.
blanco   Yo   un   tengo   béisbol.

Write three words under each category:

El salón de clase   *El campo de recreo*

_____   _____

_____   _____

_____   _____

¡Usted y Tú!
("You" and "You!")

Say *usted* to your teacher instead of *tú*.
Use *tú* only with your family and friends:

How are <u>you</u>, my friend?	*¿Cómo estás <u>tú</u>, mi amigo?*
How are <u>you</u>, teacher?	*¿Cómo está <u>usted</u>, maestro?*

Más diversión
(More Fun)

Do you have . . . ?   *¿Tienes . . . ?*

stories   *los cuentos*

tricks   *los trucos*

songs   *las canciones*

cartoons
los dibujos animados

los chistes
jokes

Let's go to the . . . **Vamos a . . .**

park **el parque**

movies or movie theater **el cine**

zoo **el zoológico**

Answer these questions by writing in SPANISH:

los chistes   los dibujos animados   los trucos

What does a magician do? _____

What do you call funny stories? _____

What do you watch on TV? _____

ANSWERS: los trucos, los chistes, los dibujos animados

Which words belong together?

**la música   el parque
los árboles   el zoológico
los leones   la canción**

ANSWERS: la música   la canción
         los árboles   el parque
         los leones   el zoológico

122

Look at this CROSSWORD puzzle. Put these words in SPANISH:

ACROSS
2. songs
3. country
4. reading
5. forest

DOWN
1. desert
2. movies
3. park

ANSWERS:

Celebremos
(Let's Celebrate)

There are many special days during the year. Here are a few in SPANISH:

Happy Birthday!	*¡Feliz cumpleaños!*
Merry Christmas!	*¡Feliz Navidad!*
Happy Easter!	*¡Felices Pascuas!*

I want the . . .	*Quiero . . .*
party	*la fiesta*
cake	*la torta*
present	*el regalo*
balloon	*el globo*

candles *las velas*

candy *los dulces*

ice cream *el helado*

Can you remember what you learned?
Write these party words in English:

los juegos y los globos _____

mi familia y mis amigos _____

la música y el baile _____

ANSWERS: the games and the balloons
my family and my friends
the music and the dancing

Answer these questions in SPANISH:

¿Cuántas velas hay en la torta? _____

¿Cuántos regalos hay en la mesa? _____

¿Cuántos globos hay en la fiesta? _____

ANSWERS: *diez, cinco, siete*

Try this conversation. But first, say what it means in English:

#1 *Hoy es mi cumpleaños.*

#2 *¡Qué bueno! ¿Cuántos años tienes?*

#1 *Tengo once. Estoy muy feliz.*

#2 *¿Hay una fiesta en tu casa?*

#1 *Sí, y vamos al cine en la noche.*

ANSWERS: #1 Today is my birthday.
#2 Great! How old are you?
#1 I'm eleven. I am very happy.
#2 Is there a party at your house?
#1 Yes, and we are going to the movies at night.

Name all your favorite snacks:

Bring . . .	*Trae . . .*
Give me . . .	*Dame . . .*
Take . . .	*Toma . . .*

pie *el pastel*

jello   *la gelatina*
cookies   *las galletas*

gum *el chicle*

popcorn *las palomitas*

peanuts *el maní*

125

Connect the words that belong together:

el helado	*las palomitas*
la música	*el frío*
la torta	*la gelatina*
el maíz	*el baile*
la fresa	*las velas*

ANSWERS: *el helado* — *la música* — *la torta* — *el maíz* — *la fresa* | *el frío* — *el baile* — *las velas* — *las palomitas* — *la gelatina*

Underline only the things you can eat:

los dulces   *los cumpleaños*   *los regalos*

las galletas   *los pasteles*   *los globos*

ANSWERS: *los dulces, las galletas, los pasteles*

Match each picture with the correct word:

el pastel

las galletas

los regalos

la torta

las palomitas

126

Say these things in SPANISH at your next party:

Welcome!	*¡Bienvenido!*
Congratulations!	*¡Felicitaciones!*
Good luck!	*¡Buena suerte!*

I hope you had fun today. Now, let's hurry home.
Are you speaking SPANISH every day?

7 CHAPTER
SIETE

De noche

(At Night)

Mucha ayuda
(A Lot of Help)

After you get home from school, help around the house.
Begin by setting the table for dinner.

Do you need help?	*¿Necesitas ayuda?*
Yes, I need the . . .	*Sí, necesito . . .*

glass   *el vaso*

plate   *el plato*

napkin   *la servilleta*

cup   *la taza*

   bowl   *el plato hondo*

saucer   *el platillo*

fork   *el tenedor*

spoon   *la cuchara*

knife   *el cuchillo*

Connect the words that go together:

la taza	*el tenedor*
la silla	*el platillo*
la cuchara	*la mesa*

Put the word that belongs on the line:

el cuchillo   *el vaso*   *el plato hondo*

Quiero _____ *de leche.*

La sopa está en _____ .

No tengo el tenedor, _____ , *y la cuchara.*

Whenever you help, add a SPANISH word to each command:

Bring . . .	*Trae . . .* _____
Give me . . .	*Dame . . .* _____
Take . . .	*Toma . . .* _____

Here's a <u>new</u> one. Fill in the blanks:

Put . . .   *Pon . . .* _____

Put the napkins there.   <u>***Pon las servilletas allí.***</u>

Put the cup on the saucer.   _____ .

Put the spoon in the bowl.   _____ .

Now, connect the sentences that mean the same:

Let's go to the kitchen.
Put the fork here.
There are six big plates.
The glass is on the table.
Look at the new cups.
I like the red napkin.
You don't have a bowl.

Mira las tazas nuevas.
Me gusta la servilleta roja.
No tienes un plato hondo.
Vamos a la cocina.
El vaso está en la mesa.
Pon el tenedor aquí.
Hay seis platos grandes.

¡La limpieza!
(Cleanup!)

After dinner, start cleaning around the house:

Use the . . .   *Usa . . .*

towel   *la toalla*
soap   *el jabón*

mop *el trapeador*

bucket *el balde*

sponge *la esponja*

Clean up with words you know. Write the English:

el agua   _____

la escoba   _____

el bote de basura   _____

Connect each question with the best answer:

¿Dónde está el agua?   En el bote de basura.
¿Dónde está el papel?   En la lavadora.
¿Dónde está la toalla?   En el balde.

Write the word to match each picture below:

1. _____   2. _____   3. _____

4. _____   5. _____

This <u>new</u> command makes cleaning easy. Can you fill in the blanks?

Clean the . . .   *Limpia . . .*

house   *la* __ __ __ __

room   *el* __ __ __ __ __ __

table   *la* __ __ __ __

Choose the right answer:

el trapeador   *la esponja*   *la escoba*

Hay tierra en la calle. Trae _____ .

Hay agua en el piso. Trae _____ .

Hay comida en la silla. Trae _____ .

Here are more things you can say:

It's clean. *Está limpia.*   It's wet. *Está mojado.*
It's dirty.   *Está sucia.*   It's dry. *Está seco.*

What do these words mean?

¿Dónde está la toalla mojada?   _____

Tengo los zapatos sucios.   _____

Mi ropero está muy limpio.   _____

Which cleaning tools always go together?
Break this code to find the answer:

1 2 3 4 5 6 7 8 9 10 11 12 13 14 15 16 17 18 19 20 21 22 23 24 25
A B C D E F G H I J K L M N O P Q R S T U V W X Y

5-12 2-1-12-4-5 25 5-12 20-18-1-16-5-1-4-15-18

ANSWERS: *el balde y el trapeador*

El baño
(The Bathroom)

Cleaning the house can be dirty work. Get washed up in the bathroom:

mirror
el espejo

toilet
el excusado

shower
la ducha

faucet *el grifo*

sink *el lavabo*

bathtub *la tina*

You know these bathroom words. Write them in SPANISH:

I like the shower.   *Me gusta* _____ .

I like the towel.   _____ .

I like the soap.   _____ .

ANSWERS: *Me gusta la ducha.*
Me gusta la toalla.
Me gusta la ducha.

134

Cross out the word that doesn't belong:

la tina, la ducha, la escuela
el grifo, el tren, el lavabo
el cuchillo, el agua, el jabón

Speak SPANISH when you turn on the water:

It's hot.   *Está caliente.*
It's cold. *Está fría.*

Color this funny picture. Then, fill in the blanks:

encima del excusado   *enfrente del espejo*   *en la ducha*

El perro está _____ .

El caballo está _____ .

El gato está _____ .

Put the words in these sentences in order, and write
what they mean in English:

mira baño la al y ducha Anda _____

lavabo Pon caliente el en agua el _____

la Toma y tina limpia esponja la _____

O.K. Stay in the bathroom, and point:

Point to the . . .   *Señala . . .*

hairbrush *el cepillo*

comb *el peine*

toothbrush *el cepillo de dientes*

toothpaste
la pasta de dientes

Underline the correct word:

Mi peine es (guapo, viejo, osito).

Pon el cepillo en el (libro, metro, baño).

El lavabo tiene un (grifo, gato, zapato).

La pasta de dientes es (camisa, alto, verde).

El espejo está (limpio, feliz, caliente).

Mi cuerpo
(My Body)

As long as you are in the bathroom, why not take a bath in SPANISH!
Say each part as you scrub:

la cabeza

el cuello

el hombro

el pecho

el estómago

el brazo

la mano

la pierna

el pie

ankle	*el tobillo*
back	*la espalda*
brain	*el cerebro*
chin	*la barbilla*
elbow	*el codo*
finger	*el dedo*
heart	*el corazón*
knee	*la rodilla*
throat	*la garganta*
wrist	*la muñeca*

In **SPANISH**, "I wash my . . . " is **Me lavo mi . . . .**
Write three things that can be washed on
the lines below:

Me lavo mi _____

Me lavo mi _____

Me lavo mi _____

Put these letters in order:

m o h o r b _____

r i n e a p _____

ó g o t e m s a _____

z a a c e b _____

l o c u l e _____

h o p e c _____

Connect the dots. What do you see—in SPANISH?

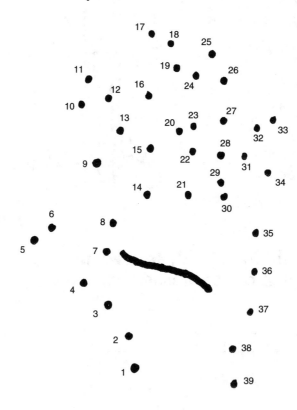

La cara
(The Face)

Every time you look into the mirror, speak SPANISH:

Look at the . . .   *Mira . . .*

Read these words as you color the girl's face:

Los ojos son azules.
El pelo es café.
Los dientes son blancos.

Here are two different monsters. What do they look like in SPANISH?

It has three eyes.   *Tiene tres ojos.*

It has two heads.   _____.

It has four arms.   _____.

139

There are four ears.   *Hay cuatro orejas.*

There are three legs.   _____ .

There are five teeth.   _____ .

Now draw this monster:

Tiene dos bocas, una nariz grande, y mucho pelo verde:

Estoy enfermo
(I'm sick.)

Talk in SPANISH when you don't feel well:

I need the . . .   *Necesito . . .*

aspirin   *la aspirina*
vitamin   *la vitamina*

medicine
la medicina

Band-aid
la curita

thermometer *el termómetro*

Circle the three words that look a lot like English:

enfermo   vitamina   curita   medicina   aspirina

ANSWERS: *vitamina, medicina, aspirina*

¿Qué te pasa? means "What's the matter?"

It's a . . .   *Es . . .*

cough   *la tos*
cold   *el resfriado*
fever   *la fiebre*

I have a . . .   *Tengo un . . .*

stomachache   *dolor de estómago*
headache   *dolor de cabeza*
toothache   *dolor de muela*

141

Connect the words that belong together:

dolor de cabeza   el dentista
dolor de estómago   la aspirina
dolor de muela   la comida

Practice, and then write these words in English:

#1 ¿Qué te pasa? ¿Estás enfermo?

_____

#2 Sí. Tengo dolor de cabeza y fiebre.

_____

#1 ¿Quieres un doctor?

_____

#2 No, gracias. Necesito un termómetro y aspirina.

_____

A la cama
(Off to Bed)

It's bedtime, so . . . **anda a la cama.**

Are you all tucked in? **¡Muy bien!** Now, look out the window and talk about the sky at night:

Look at the . . .   **Mira . . .**

constellation   **la constelación**
star   **la estrella**   planet
moon   **la luna**   **el planeta**
space   **el espacio**

comet **el cometa**

Put different words on the lines below. Then, read in SPANISH:

Señala _____ .

Me gusta _____ .

Vamos a _____ .

Color these things:

Tres planetas verdes, cafés y azules

Una estrella amarilla

Dos lunas blancas

Dime un cuento
(Tell me a story.)

Before you fall asleep, take out your favorite storybook.
Name these characters *en español*:

It is the . . .   *Es . . .*

princess   *la princesa*
fairy   *la hada*

wizard *el mago*

king *el rey*

elf *el duende*

144

Here is the . . . *Aquí tienes . . .*

ghost   *el fantasma*
giant   *el gigante*

witch
la bruja

monster
el monstruo

dragon
el dragón

Answer with **T** for TRUE and **F** for FALSE:

El duende es más grande que el gigante. _____

La hija del rey es la princesa. _____

Las brujas son muy bonitas. _____

There is a secret character hidden below. Circle every other letter to find out who it is:

O S T O L Y O C A H S I A C M O O Y I T

T E N N E G R O S L K A O S B O A R F E

O J O A L S I G A R N A S N O D E E P S

What's the secret message? _____

Which character am I? _____

Draw a line from these words to each picture:

La bruja tiene su escoba.

La princesa está muy triste.

El fantasma está en la casa.

Soon it will be morning. When you wake up, turn to Chapter One, and read this book again!

Hablo español
(I Speak Spanish)

Have you learned all the words in this book?

¡Qué bueno!

Now—from the time you get up until the time you go to bed— you can really speak . . .

. . . SPANISH every day!

Powerful Practice Tips

1. When you come to a new Spanish word, be sure to read it three times—aloud!

2. Touch and name all the pictures in this book. Then, color everything you can.

3. Do all the activities in each chapter, and don't forget to check your answers.

4. Use the flashcards at the back of this book. Go slowly, and learn one group of words at a time.

5. If you can, try out new words with real Spanish speakers. Otherwise, practice with a family member or friend.

6. Look for Spanish-speaking programs on your TV or Internet channels. The more you listen to Spanish, the more you will learn!

7. If you purchased the book and CD package: Read only a few pages at a time. And, before you move forward, stop the CD, replay it, and read the pages again!

Here's the best way to practice SPANISH EVERY DAY.
Just check off what you do on the list below.

My Daily Checklist

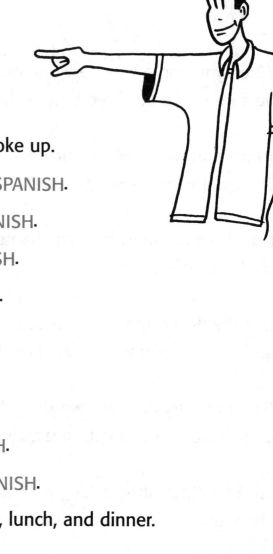

- [ ] I spoke SPANISH right after I woke up.

- [ ] I used a friendly expression in SPANISH.

- [ ] I practiced my numbers in SPANISH.

- [ ] I played with my toys in SPANISH.

- [ ] I put on my clothes in SPANISH.

- [ ] I used a command in SPANISH.

- [ ] I said some colors in SPANISH.

- [ ] I asked a question in SPANISH.

- [ ] I spoke to my family in SPANISH.

- [ ] I talked about my home in SPANISH.

- [ ] I spoke in SPANISH at breakfast, lunch, and dinner.

- [ ] I gave the time in SPANISH.

- [ ] I said the day and date in SPANISH.

- [ ] I talked about my school in SPANISH.

- [ ] I played games with my friends in SPANISH.

Spanish Culture

People who live in Spanish-speaking countries do some things differently from what we do in the United States. That is because they have a different culture. A culture includes things like the way people live, what they eat, and how they dress. You can learn more about culture in books or on the Internet. But, the best way to learn about people is to talk to them. When you get the chance, talk to as many Spanish-speaking people as you can. Soon you will know more than the Spanish language—you will understand the culture, too!

A Spanish Song

Do you know the tune
to "Are you sleeping"?

Here's how people
sing it in Spanish:

Mar-ti-ni-llo, Mar-ti-ni-llo,
(mahr-tee-nee-yoh)

¿duer-mes tú? ¿duer-mes tú?
(dwehr-mehs too)

Sue-na la cam-pa-na, sue-na la cam-pa-na;
(sweh-nah lah kahm-pah-nah)

Din-din-don, din-din-don.
(deen-deen-dohn)

ENGLISH TRANSLATION:
Martinillo, Martinillo,
Are you sleeping? Are you sleeping?
The bell is ringing, the bell is ringing;
Ding-ding-dong, ding-ding-dong.

Vocabulary List

ENGLISH	ESPAÑOL
a	*un* or *una*
a little	*poca* or *poco*
a lot	*mucha* or *mucho*
above	*encima*
address	*la dirección*
after	*después*
all	*toda* or *todo*
almost	*casi*
always	*siempre*
American	*americana* or *americano*
an	*un* or *una*
and	*y*
angel	*el ángel*
angry	*enojada* or *enojado*
animal	*el animal*
another	*otra* or *otro*
ant	*la hormiga*
apartment	*el apartamento*
apple	*la manzana*
April	*abril*
arm	*el brazo*
armchair	*el sillón*
art	*el arte*
aspirin	*la aspirina*
astronaut	*el astronauta*
at	*en*
attic	*el desván*
August	*agosto*

aunt	*la tía*
baby	*el bebé*
back	*la espalda*
backpack	*la mochila*
bad	*mala* or *malo*
bag	*la bolsa*
ball	*la pelota*
balloon	*el globo*
banana	*el plátano*
Band-aid	*la curita*
bank	*el banco*
bars	*las barras*
baseball	*el béisbol*
basement	*el sótano*
basketball	*el baloncesto*
bat	*el bate*
bathroom	*el baño*
bathtub	*la tina*
beach	*la playa*
beans	*los frijoles*
bed	*la cama*
bedroom	*el dormitorio*
bedspread	*la cubrecama*
bee	*la abeja*
before	*antes*
behind	*detrás*
bell	*la campana*
belt	*el cinturón*
benches	*los bancos*
bicycle	*la bicicleta*
big	*grande*
bird	*el pájaro*
black	*negra* or *negro*
blanket	*la frazada*
blocks	*los bloques*
blouse	*la blusa*
blue	*azul*
boat	*el bote*

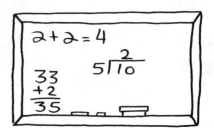

body	*el cuerpo*
book	*el libro*
bookshelf	*el librero*
boots	*las botas*
bottle	*la botella*
bowl	*el plato hondo*
boy	*el niño*
bracelet	*el brazalete*
brave	*valiente*
bread	*el pan*
breakfast	*el desayuno*
bridge	*el puente*
broom	*la escoba*
brother	*el hermano*
brown	*café*
bucket	*el balde*
building	*el edificio*
bulletin board	*el tablero de anuncios*
bus	*el autobús*
bush	*el arbusto*
but	*pero*
butter	*la mantequilla*
cabinet	*el gabinete*
cake	*la torta*
calendar	*el calendario*
camera	*la cámara*
candles	*las velas*
candy	*los dulces*
cap	*la gorra*
car	*el carro*
carpet	*la alfombra*
carrot	*la zanahoria*
cartoons	*los dibujos animados*
cat	*la gata* or *el gato*
ceiling	*el techo*
celery	*el apio*
chair	*la silla*

chalk	*la tiza*
chapter	*el capítulo*
cheap	*barata* or *barato*
checkers	*el juego de damas*
cheese	*el queso*
chest	*el pecho*
chicken	*el pollo*
children	*los niños*
chimney	*la chimenea*
chocolate	*el chocolate*
church	*la iglesia*
city	*la ciudad*
class	*la clase*
classroom	*el salón de clase*
clean	*limpia* or *limpio*
clock	*el reloj*
closed	*cerrada* or *cerrado*
closet	*el ropero*
clothes	*la ropa*
cloudy	*nublada* or *nublado*
clown	*el payaso*
cockroach	*la cucaracha*
coffee	*el café*
coin	*la moneda*
cold (flu)	*el resfriado*
cold (temperature)	*fría* or *frío*
color	*el color*
comb	*el peine*
comet	*el cometa*
computer	*la computadora*
cook	*el cocinero*
cookies	*las galletas*
corn	*el maíz*
corner	*la esquina*
couch	*el sofá*
cough	*la tos*
country	*el país*

cousin	*la prima* or *el primo*
cow	*la vaca*
crayons	*los gises*
crazy	*loca* or *loco*
cup	*la taza*
curtains	*las cortinas*
dancing	*el baile*
dangerous	*peligrosa* or *peligroso*
dark	*oscura* or *oscuro*
daughter	*la hija*
day	*el día*
December	*diciembre*
deer	*el venado*
dentist	*la* or *el dentista*
desert	*el desierto*
desk	*el escritorio*
dessert	*el postre*
different	*diferente*
difficult	*difícil*
dining room	*el comedor*
dinner	*la cena*
dinosaur	*el dinosaurio*
dirt	*la tierra*
dirty	*sucia* or *sucio*
dishes	*la loza*
doctor	*la doctora* or *el doctor*
dog	*la perra* or *el perro*
doll	*la muñeca*
dollar	*el dólar*
donkey	*la burra* or *el burro*
door	*la puerta*
down	*abajo*
dragon	*el dragón*
drawing	*el dibujo*
dress	*el vestido*
dresser	*el tocador*
drinks	*las bebidas*

drum	*el tambor*
dry	*seca* or *seco*
dryer	*la secadora*
duck	*la pata* or *el pato*
each	*cada*
ear	*la oreja*
early	*temprano*
earrings	*los aretes*
easy	*fácil*
egg	*el huevo*
eight	*ocho*
eighteen	*dieciocho*
eighty	*ochenta*
elephant	*la elefanta* or *el elefante*
elevator	*el ascensor*
eleven	*once*
elf	*el duende*
empty	*vacía* or *vacío*
end	*el fin*
engine	*el motor*
English	*el inglés*
enough	*bastante*
envelope	*el sobre*
eraser	*el borrador*
everybody	*todas* or *todos*
excellent	*excelente*
excited	*emocionada* or *emocionado*
expensive	*cara* or *caro*
eye	*el ojo*
face	*la cara*
factory	*la fábrica*
fairy	*la hada*
fall	*el otoño*
family	*la familia*
fantastic	*fantástica* or *fantástico*
far	*lejos*
farm	*la finca*

fat	*gorda* or *gordo*
father	*el padre*
fast	*rápida* or *rápido*
faucet	*el grifo*
favorite	*favorita* or *favorito*
feather	*la pluma*
February	*febrero*
fence	*la cerca*
fever	*la fiebre*
few	*poca* or *poco*
fifteen	*quince*
fifty	*cincuenta*
fine	*bien*
firefighter	*el bombero*
first	*primera* or *primero*
fish	*el pez* or *el pescado* (out of the water)
five	*cinco*
flag	*la bandera*
floor	*el piso*
flower	*la flor*
fly	*la mosca*
food	*la comida*
foot	*el pie*
for	*para*
forest	*el bosque*
fork	*el tenedor*
forty	*cuarenta*
four	*cuatro*
fourteen	*catorce*
french fries	*las papas fritas*
Friday	*viernes*
friend	*la amiga* or *el amigo*
from	*de*
fruit	*la fruta*
frying pan	*el sartén*
full	*llena* or *lleno*
fun	*la diversión*

funny	*chistosa* or *chistoso*
furniture	*los muebles*
game	*el juego*
garage	*el garaje*
garden	*el jardín*
gas station	*la gasolinera*
gate	*el portón*
ghost	*el fantasma*
giant	*el gigante*
giraffe	*la jirafa*
girl	*la niña*
glass	*el vaso*
glove	*el guante*
glue	*el pegamento*
God	*Díos*
good	*buena* or *bueno*
good-bye	*adiós*
grandfather	*el abuelo*
grandmother	*la abuela*
grape	*la uva*
grass	*el pasto*
gray	*gris*
green	*verde*
guitar	*la guitarra*
gum	*el chicle*
hair	*el pelo*
hairbrush	*el cepillo*
haircut	*el corte de pelo*
hallway	*el pasillo*
ham	*el jamón*
hamburger	*la hamburguesa*
hammer	*el martillo*
hand	*la mano*
handkerchief	*el pañuelo*
handsome	*guapo*
happy	*feliz*
hard	*dura* or *duro*

has	*tiene*
he	*él*
he is	*él es*
head	*la cabeza*
headache	*el dolor de cabeza*
heart	*el corazón*
helicopter	*el helicóptero*
hello	*hola*
her	*su*
here	*aquí*
highway	*la carretera*
hill	*el cerro*
his	*su*
homework	*la tarea*
honey	*la miel*
horn	*la trompeta*
horse	*el caballo*
hose	*la manguera*
hospital	*el hospital*
hot	*caliente*
hot dog	*el perro caliente*
hotel	*el hotel*
hour	*la hora*
house	*la casa*
hug	*el abrazo*
husband	*esposo*
I	*yo*
I am	*yo estoy* or *yo soy*
ice	*el hielo*
ice cream	*el helado*
important	*importante*
in front	*enfrente*
in	*en*
insect	*el insecto*
inside	*adentro*
it is	*es* or *está*
jacket	*la chaqueta*
January	*enero*

jello	*la gelatina*
joke	*el chiste*
juice	*el jugo*
July	*julio*
June	*junio*
key	*la llave*
king	*el rey*
kiss	*el beso*
kitchen	*la cocina*
kite	*la cometa*
kitty	*el gatito*
knife	*el cuchillo*
ladder	*la escalera*
lady (Mrs.)	*Señora (Sra.)*
lake	*el lago*
lamp	*la lámpara*
language	*el lenguaje*
last	*última* or *último*
late	*tarde*
later	*luego*
lazy	*perezosa* or *perezoso*
leaf	*la hoja*
left	*izquierda*
leg	*la pierna*
lemonade	*la limonada*
less	*menos*
lettuce	*la lechuga*
library	*la biblioteca*
lights	*las luces*
lion	*la leona* or *el león*
little	*chica* or *chico*
living room	*la sala*
long	*larga* or *largo*
love	*el amor*
lunch	*el almuerzo*
magazine	*la revista*
magic	*la magia*

mail	*el correo*
mail carrier	*el cartero*
mailbox	*el buzón*
man	*el hombre*
many	*muchas* or *muchos*
map	*el mapa*
March	*marzo*
marker	*el marcador*
math	*las matemáticas*
May	*mayo*
meat	*la carne*
mechanic	*el* or *la mecánico*
medicine	*la medicina*
merry-go-round	*los caballitos*
milk	*la leche*
milk shake	*el batido*
minute	*el minuto*
mirror	*el espejo*
Miss (Ms.)	*Señorita (Srta.)*
Mister (Mr.)	*Señor (Sr.)*
Monday	*lunes*
money	*el dinero*
monster	*el monstruo*
month	*el mes*
moon	*la luna*
mop	*el trapeador*
more	*más*
morning	*la mañana*
mother	*la madre*
motorcycle	*la motocicleta*
mountain	*la montaña*
mouse	*el ratón*
mouth	*la boca*
movies	*el cine*
mud	*el lodo*
music	*la música*
my	*mi*

nail	*el clavo*
name	*el nombre*
napkin	*la servilleta*
near	*cerca*
necessary	*necesaria* or *necesario*
neck	*el cuello*
necklace	*el collar*
neighbor	*el vecino*
never	*nunca*
new	*nueva* or *nuevo*
newspaper	*el periódico*
nice	*simpática* or *simpático*
night	*la noche*
nine	*nueve*
nineteen	*diecinueve*
ninety	*noventa*
no	*no*
nobody	*nadie*
none	*ninguna* or *ninguno*
nose	*la nariz*
not	*no*
notebook	*el cuaderno*
nothing	*nada*
November	*noviembre*
now	*ahora*
number	*el número*
nurse	*la enfermera* or *el enfermero*
October	*octubre*
of	*de*
office	*la oficina*
old	*vieja* or *viejo*
on	*en*
one	*uno*
one hundred	*cien*
one thousand	*mil*
onion	*la cebolla*
only	*sólo* or *solamente*

open	*abierta* or *abierto*
or	*o*
orange (color)	*anaranjada* or *anaranjado*
orange (fruit)	*la naranja*
our	*nuestra* or *nuestro*
outside	*afuera*
overcoat	*el abrigo*
page	*la página*
paint	*la pintura*
pajamas	*el pijama*
pants	*los pantalones*
paper	*el papel*
parents	*los padres*
park	*el parque*
party	*la fiesta*
peanut	*el maní*
pen	*el lapicero*
pencil	*el lápiz*
pencil sharpener	*el sacapuntas*
people	*la gente*
pepper	*la pimienta*
person	*la persona*
pet	*el animal doméstico*
phone number	*el número de teléfono*
photo	*la foto*
pie	*el pastel*
pig	*el puerco*
pillow	*la almohada*
pilot	*la* or *el piloto*
pink	*rosada* or *rosado*
place	*el lugar*
plane	*el avión*
planet	*el planeta*
plant	*la planta*
plate	*el plato*
playground	*el campo de recreo*
please	*por favor*

pliers	*las pinzas*
police	*la policía*
police officer	*el policía*
pool	*la piscina*
poor	*pobre*
popcorn	*las palomitas*
possible	*posible*
post office	*la oficina de correo*
pot	*la olla*
potato	*la papa*
present	*el regalo*
pretty	*bonita* or *bonito*
prince	*el príncipe*
princess	*la princesa*
proud	*orgullosa* or *orgulloso*
puppy	*la perrita* or *el perrito*
purple	*morada* or *morado*
purse	*la bolsa*
puzzle	*el rompecabezas*
queen	*la reina*
rabbit	*la coneja* or *el conejo*
radio	*el radio*
rain	*la lluvia*
raincoat	*el impermeable*
rake	*el rastrillo*
reading	*la lectura*
red	*roja* or *rojo*
refrigerator	*el refrigerador*
restaurant	*el restaurante*
restroom	*el servicio*
ribbon	*la cinta*
rice	*el arroz*
rich	*rica* or *rico*
right	*derecha* or *derecho*
ring	*el anillo*
river	*el río*
road	*el camino*
robot	*el robot*

rock	*la roca*
rocket	*el cohete*
room	*el cuarto*
sad	*triste*
salad	*la ensalada*
salesperson	*la vendedora* or *el vendedor*
salt	*la sal*
same	*misma* or *mismo*
sandwich	*el sandwich*
Saturday	*sábado*
saucer	*el platillo*
sausage	*la salchicha*
saw	*el serrucho*
scarf	*la bufanda*
school	*la escuela*
science	*la ciencia*
scissors	*las tijeras*
screwdriver	*el destornillador*
sea	*el mar*
second	*el segundo*
secretary	*la secretaria* or *el secretario*
seesaw	*el subibaja*
September	*septiembre*
seven	*siete*
seventeen	*diecisiete*
seventy	*setenta*
shampoo	*el champú*
she	*ella*
she is	*ella es*
sheep	*la oveja*
sheet	*la sábana*
ship	*el barco*
shirt	*la camisa*
shoes	*los zapatos*
short	*baja* or *bajo*
shorts	*los pantalones cortos*
shoulder	*el hombro*
shovel	*la pala*

shower	*la ducha*
side	*el lado*
sidewalk	*la acera*
sign	*el letrero*
sink	*el lavabo*
sister	*la hermana*
six	*seis*
sixteen	*dieciséis*
sixty	*sesenta*
size	*el tamaño*
skateboard	*la patineta*
skates	*los patines*
skirt	*la falda*
slide	*el resbalador*
slippers	*las pantuflas*
slow	*lenta* or *lento*
smart	*inteligente*
smile	*la sonrisa*
snail	*el caracol*
snake	*la culebra*
snow	*la nieve*
soap	*el jabón*
soccer	*el fútbol*
social studies	*los estudios sociales*
socks	*los calcetines*
soda	*el refresco*
soldier	*el soldado*
some	*algunas* or *algunos*
someone	*alguien*
something	*algo*
sometimes	*a veces*
son	*el hijo*
song	*la canción*
soon	*pronto*
soup	*la sopa*
space	*el espacio*
spaceship	*la nave espacial*
Spanish	*el español*

special	*especial*
spider	*la araña*
sponge	*la esponja*
spoon	*la cuchara*
sports	*los deportes*
spring	*la primavera*
stairs	*las escaleras*
stapler	*la engrapadora*
star	*la estrella*
state	*el estado*
steak	*el bistec*
stereo	*el estéreo*
stomach	*el estómago*
stomachache	*el dolor de estómago*
stone	*la piedra*
store	*la tienda*
story	*el cuento*
stove	*la estufa*
strawberry	*la fresa*
street	*la calle*
strong	*fuerte*
student	*la* or *el estudiante*
stuffed animal	*el animal de peluche*
subway	*el metro*
sugar	*el azúcar*
suit	*el traje*
Sunday	*domingo*
supermarket	*el supermercado*
sweater	*el suéter*
sweet	*dulce*
swing	*el columpio*
table	*la mesa*
tall	*alta* or *alto*
tasty	*sabrosa* or *sabroso*
tea	*el té*
teacher	*la maestra* or *el maestro*
team	*el equipo*
teddy bear	*el osito*

teeth	*los dientes*
telephone	*el teléfono*
television	*el televisor*
ten	*diez*
thanks	*gracias*
that	*esa* or *eso*
the	*el, la, los, las*
their	*su*
then	*entonces*
there	*allí*
thermometer	*el termómetro*
these	*estas* or *estos*
they are	*ellos están* or *ellos son*
thin	*delgada* or *delgado*
thing	*la cosa*
third	*tercera* or *tercero*
thirteen	*trece*
thirty	*treinta*
this	*esta* or *este*
those	*esas* or *esos*
throat	*la garganta*
three	*tres*
Thursday	*jueves*
tie	*la corbata*
tiger	*el tigre*
time	*el tiempo*
tired	*cansada* or *cansado*
to	*a*
to the	*al*
today	*hoy*
together	*juntas* or *juntos*
toilet	*el excusado*
tomato	*el tomate*
tomorrow	*mañana*
tool	*la herramienta*
toothache	*el dolor de muela*
toothbrush	*el cepillo de dientes*

toothpaste	*la pasta de dientes*
towel	*la toalla*
town	*el pueblo*
toy	*el juguete*
traffic light	*el semáforo*
train	*el tren*
trash can	*el bote de basura*
tree	*el árbol*
tricks	*los trucos*
truck	*el camión*
t-shirt	*la camiseta*
Tuesday	*martes*
turkey	*el pavo*
turtle	*la tortuga*
twelve	*doce*
twenty	*veinte*
two	*dos*
ugly	*fea* or *feo*
umbrella	*el paraguas*
uncle	*el tío*
under	*bajo* or *abajo*
underwear	*la ropa interior*
United States	*Estados Unidos*
up	*arriba*
vacation	*las vacaciones*
vacuum cleaner	*la aspiradora*
vegetables	*los vegetales*
very	*muy*
videos	*los vídeos*
vitamin	*la vitamina*
waiter	*el mesero*
wall	*la pared*
wallet	*la cartera*
washer	*la lavadora*
watch	*el reloj*
water	*el agua*
watermelon	*la sandía*

we	*nosotras* or *nosotros*
weak	*débil*
weather	*el tiempo*
Wednesday	*miércoles*
week	*la semana*
wet	*mojado* or *mojada*
white	*blanca* or *blanco*
whiteboard	*el pizarrón*
wife	*la esposa*
window	*la ventana*
winter	*el invierno*
witch	*la bruja*
with	*con*
without	*sin*
wizard	*el mago*
woman	*la mujer*
word	*la palabra*
work	*el trabajo*
worker	*la trabajadora* or *el trabajador*
world	*el mundo*
worm	*el gusano*
yard	*el patio*
year	*el año*
yellow	*amarillo*
yes	*sí*
yesterday	*ayer*
you *(formal)*	*usted*
you *(informal)*	*tú*
you are	*tú eres* or *tú estás*
you guys	*ustedes*
young	*joven*
young person	*muchacha* or *muchacho*
your	*tu*
zero	*cero*
zoo	*el zoológico*

Expressions

ENGLISH	ESPAÑOL
And you?	¿Y tú?
At night.	De noche.
At__o'clock	A las ___.
Congratulations!	¡Felicitaciones!
Do you have __?	¿Tienes ___?
Do you know?	¿Sabes?
Do you like it?	¿Te gusta?
Do you need help?	¿Necesitas ayuda?
Do you speak Spanish?	¿Hablas español?
Do you understand?	¿Entiendes?
Do you want __?	¿Quieres ___?
Excuse me.	Con permiso.
Good afternoon.	Buenas tardes.
Good luck!	¡Buena suerte!
Good morning.	Buenos días.
Good night.	Buenas noches.
Happy Birthday!	¡Feliz cumpleaños!
Happy Easter!	¡Felices Pascuas!
Hi!	¡Hola!
How are you?	¿Cómo estás?
How many?	¿Cuántos?
How much?	¿Cuánto?
How old are you?	¿Cuántos años tienes?
How pretty!	¡Qué bonito!
How?	¿Cómo?
How's the weather?	¿Qué tiempo hace?
I don't know.	No sé.

I don't remember.	*No recuerdo.*
I don't understand.	*No entiendo.*
I have it.	*Lo tengo.*
I like it.	*Me gusta.*
I live at __.	*Vivo en ___.*
I need the __.	*Necesito ___.*
I put on the __.	*Me pongo ___.*
I speak a little.	*Hablo un poquito.*
I take off the __.	*Me quito ___.*
I want the __.	*Quiero ___.*
I'm hungry.	*Tengo hambre.*
I'm learning Spanish.	*Estoy aprendiendo español.*
I'm sick.	*Estoy enferma* or *Estoy enfermo.*
I'm sorry.	*Lo siento.*
I'm thirsty.	*Tengo sed.*
It's __ o'clock.	*Son las ___.*
It's cold.	*Hace frío.*
It's hot.	*Hace calor.*
It's raining.	*Está lloviendo.*
It's snowing.	*Está nevando.*
It's sunny.	*Hace sol.*
Let's celebrate.	*Celebremos.*
Let's go to the __.	*Vamos a ___.*
Me, too.	*Yo tambien.*
Merry Christmas!	*¡Feliz Navidad!*
My name is __.	*Me llamo ___.*
Not much.	*Sin novedad.*
See you later.	*Hasta luego.*
Speak more slowly.	*Habla más despacio.*
Sure.	*Claro.*
Thanks a lot.	*Muchas gracias.*
There is/are __.	*Hay ___.*
Very well.	*Muy bien.*
Welcome!	*¡Bienvenidos!*
What color is it?	*¿De qué color es?*
What grade are you in?	*¿En qué grado estás?*
What time is it?	*¿Qué hora es?*

Muchas gracias.

What?	*¿Qué?*
What's going on?	*¿Qué pasa?*
What's the date?	*¿Cuál es la fecha?*
What's the matter?	*¿Qué te pasa?*
What's your name?	*¿Cómo te llamas?*
When?	*¿Cuándo?*
Where?	*¿Dónde?*
Where do you live?	*¿Dónde vives?*
Where is it?	*¿Dónde está?*
Which?	*¿Cuál?*
Who?	*¿Quién?*
Why?	*¿Por qué?*
You're welcome.	*De nada.*

De nada.

Commands

ENGLISH	ESPAÑOL
Clean.	*Limpia.*
Come.	*Ven.*
Give me.	*Dame.*
Go.	*Anda.*
Look at.	*Mira.*
Point to.	*Señala.*
Take.	*Toma.*
Bring.	*Trae.*
Eat.	*Come.*
Drink.	*Bebe.*
Put.	*Pon.*
Tell me.	*Díme.*
Touch.	*Toca.*
Use.	*Usa.*
Wash.	*Lava.*

ENGLISH-SPANISH FLASHCARDS

Use scissors to cut along the dotted lines. Keep the cards together with a rubber band, and put them in a safe place, so you can take them out whenever you want to practice. Start right now!

la lámpara

la silla

el tocador

el reloj

el ropero

la mesa

lamp

la lampara

chair

dresser

clock

closet

table

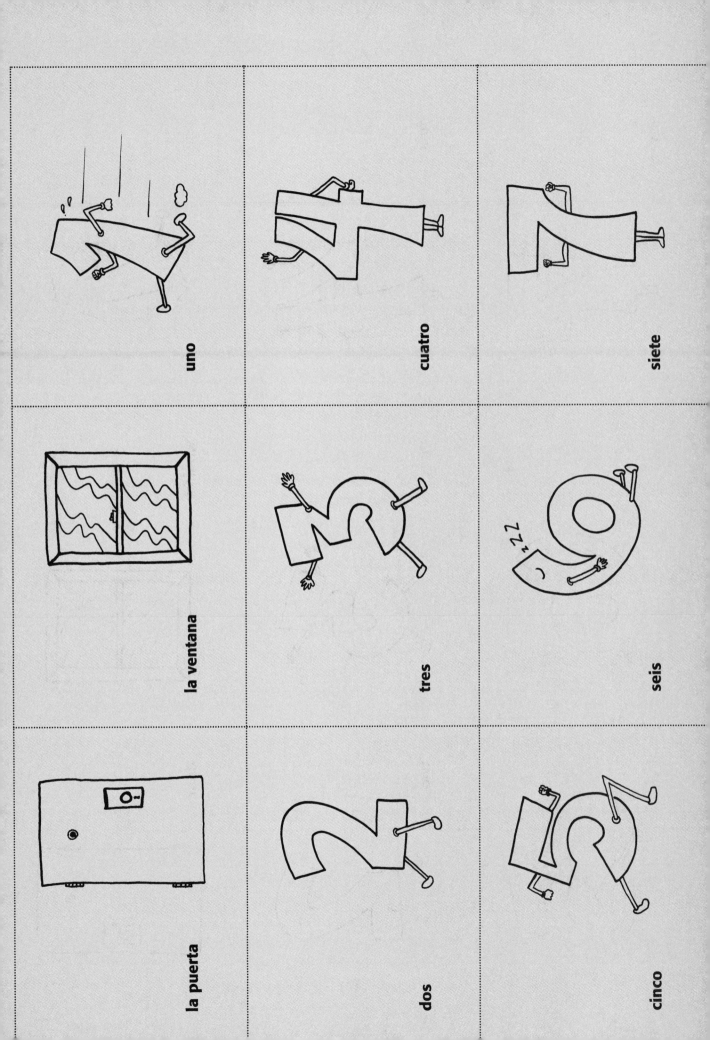

uno

la ventana

la puerta

cuatro

tres

dos

siete

seis

cinco

seven

four

one

six

three

window

five

two

door

diez

el juguete

el tren

nueve

doce

la muñeca

ocho

once

el rompecabezas

train

toy

ten

doll

twelve

nine

puzzle

eleven

eight

el carro

el soldado

la bicicleta

el barco

la pelota

la patineta

el camión

el bate

la guitarra

car	ship	truck
soldier	ball	bat
bicycle	skateboard	guitar

los calcetines

la falda

el suéter

el traje

los pantalones

el cinturón

la computadora

la camisa

el vestido

sweater

skirt

socks

belt

pants

suit

dress

shirt

computer

madre
esposa

hermana
hija

grande

el zapato

hermano
hijo

abuelo

la chaqueta

padre
esposo

abuela

mother
wife

shoe

jacket

sister
daughter

brother
son

father
husband

big

grandfather

grandmother

delgado

feo

viejo

alto

bonita

limpio

chico

gordo

sucio

old

ugly

thin

clean

pretty

tall

dirty

fat

little

lleno

hace frío

hace calor

barato

caro

vacío

el escritorio

el sofá

la alfombra

desk

cheap

full

couch

expensive

it's cold

carpet

empty

it's hot

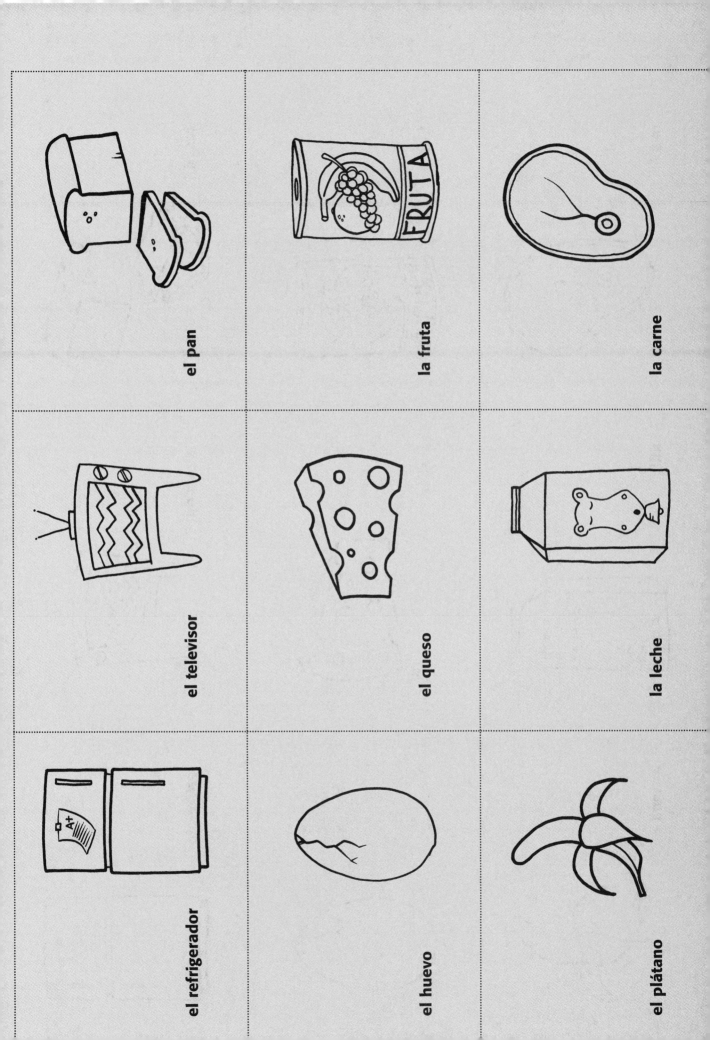

el pan

la fruta

la carne

el televisor

el queso

la leche

el refrigerador

el huevo

el plátano

meat

fruit

FRUTA

bread

milk

cheese

television

banana

egg

refrigerator

A+

la papa

el pollo

el árbol

la naranja

el maíz

el refresco

la manzana

el tomate

el pescado

tree

chicken

potato

soda

corn

orange

fish

tomato

apple

el pájaro

la calle

el restaurante

el gato

el autobús

el edificio

el perro

la ciudad

el semáforo

bird

cat

dog

street

bus

city

restaurant

building

traffic light

Restaurante La Habana

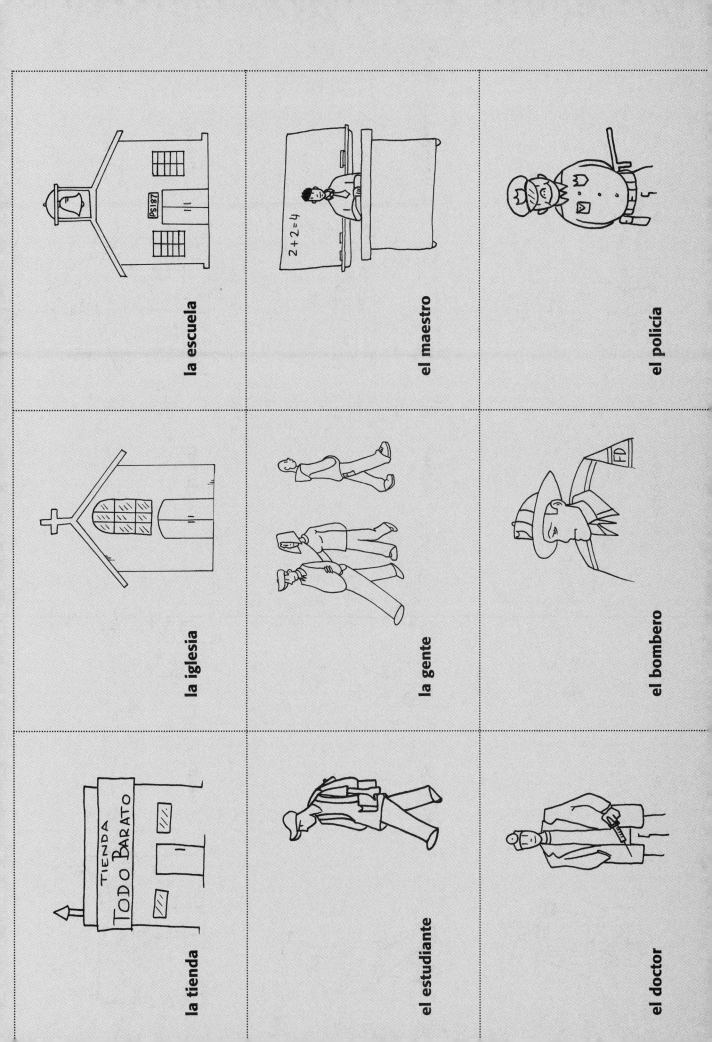

la tienda

la iglesia

la escuela

el estudiante

la gente

el maestro

el doctor

el bombero

el policía

police officer

teacher

school

firefighter

people

church

doctor

student

store

el cartero

los bancos

el lapicero

el mesero

la campana

el lápiz

el mecánico

el pizarrón

el papel

pen

benches

mail carrier

pencil

bell

waiter

paper

whiteboard

mechanic

$$2 + 2 = 4$$

$$\begin{array}{r} 33 \\ + 2 \\ \hline 35 \end{array}$$

$$5\overline{)10}^{\,2}$$

el columpio

el baile

el cine

los gises

la lectura

las canciones

el cuaderno

el fútbol

los dibujos
animados

movie theater

dancing

swing

songs

reading

crayons

cartoons

soccer

notebook

la torta

los regalos

el plato

la fiesta

los dulces

las galletas

el zoológico

el helado

el pastel

plate	cookies	pie

presents	candy	ice cream

cake	party	zoo

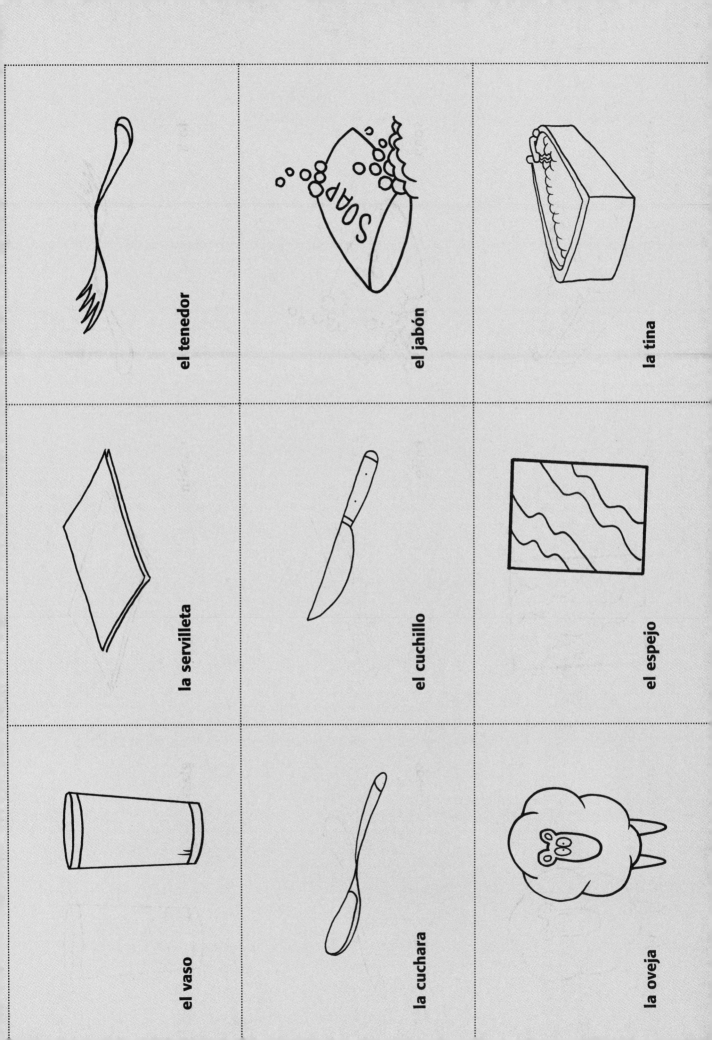

el tenedor

el jabón

la tina

la servilleta

el cuchillo

el espejo

el vaso

la cuchara

la oveja

fork

soap

SOAP

bathtub

napkin

knife

mirror

glass

spoon

sheep

la noche

la nave espacial

el libro

el peine

la luna

el juguete

el cepillo

la estrella
el sol

la cama

book

spaceship

night

toy

moon

comb

bed

star
sun

hairbrush

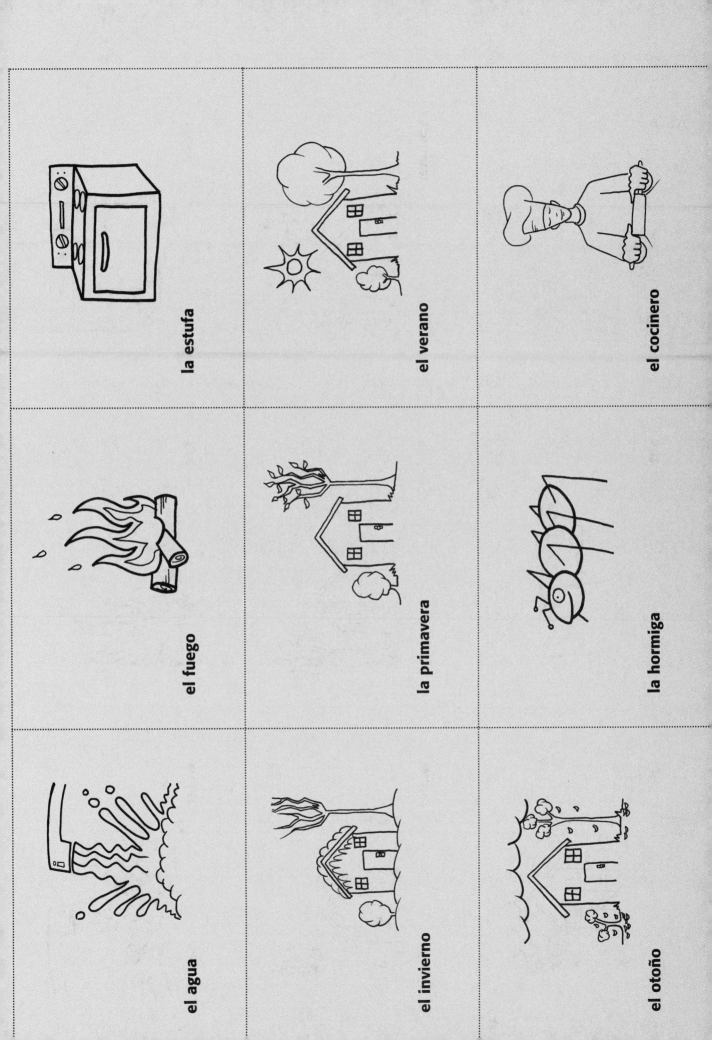

la estufa

el verano

el cocinero

el fuego

la primavera

la hormiga

el agua

el invierno

el otoño

cook

summer

stove

ant

spring

fire

fall

winter

water